raise your voice

raise your voice

A STUDENT GUIDE TO MAKING POSITIVE SOCIAL CHANGE

Editors:

Richard E. Cone

Abby Kiesa

Nicholas V. Longo

Campus Compact

inside you'll find

vii About the Editors

1 Introduction

7 Chapter 1
Lessons Learned on the Road to Student Civic Engagement

45 Chapter 2
Community Mapping on Campus

55 Chapter 3
Civic Dialogues

105 Chapter 4
Connecting Service and Political Engagement

139 Appendix
Training the Trainers

About the Editors

Richard E. Cone was the director of the University of Southern California Joint Educational Project (JEP) from 1980 until 2002. JEP is an academically based service-learning program involving more than 1,600 undergraduates each year. Recognized as a pioneer in the national service-learning movement, Dick has been engaged in Campus Compact activities since 1987. In 1999, he received California Campus Compact's Richard E. Cone Award for Community-Higher Education Partnerships. In 2000 USC received recognition as "College of the Year 1999–2000" for its work in the community, in part because of JEP's efforts under Dick's direction. After retiring from USC, Dick worked on Campus Compact's national Raise Your Voice civic engagement campaign and served as a consultant to colleges and universities. He is now a woodworker.

Abby Kiesa is the youth coordinator at the Center for Information and Research on Civic Learning and Engagement (CIRCLE), where she serves as a liaison to practitioner organizations across the country. She works to ensure that educators, youth-serving programs, and young people can use civic engagement research as a tool to strengthen and support youth engagement. Previously Abby co-directed Campus Compact's national Raise Your Voice campaign; before that, she advised student-led community partnerships at the University of Virginia's Madison House. She holds a sociology degree from Villanova University, where, as a student, she co-created two service-learning courses and a leadership development program within the Center for Peace & Justice Education.

Nicholas V. Longo is a program officer at the Kettering Foundation in the area of civic education. From 2002 to 2004, Nick directed Campus Compact's national youth civic engagement initiative, Raise Your Voice, a multiyear campaign to increase college student participation in public life. Nick co-edited *Students as Colleagues: Expanding the Circle of Service-Learning Leadership* (Campus Compact, 2006). He is also the author of *Reaching Beyond the Schools* on the role of community in creating democratic citizens (forthcoming, SUNY Press). Over the past four years, he has conducted more than 50 workshops designed to help students be more effective organizers. Nick received his Ph.D. in education from the University of Minnesota in 2005.

A Note on Volume Contributors

Contributors to this volume include Raise Your Voice Student Fellows **Tara Germond, Ellen Love, Liz Moran, Sherita Moses,** and **Stephanie Raill,** who wrote the text for Chapter 1; **Sarah Seames,** a Youth Engaged in Service Ambassador at Maine Campus Compact, who wrote sections of Chapter 4; and all of the Raise Your Voice student leaders around the country who tested and refined the tools and ideas presented here.

Introduction

The title of the wonderful book documenting conversations between legendary community educators Myles Horton and Paulo Freire (1991) sums up the idea behind this guide: *We Make the Road by Walking*. During the past three years, students on hundreds of campuses in more than 30 states have been organizing to effect change through Raise Your Voice, a nonpartisan, student-led civic initiative sponsored by Campus Compact and funded by The Pew Charitable Trusts. This guide gathers some of the lessons and tools from the road these student leaders have paved through their efforts to make campuses more free and democratic spaces. It is meant for students who want to be change agents on campus and in their communities. It provides advice for experienced student organizers looking for inspiration as well as ideas for students who may be active in community service but are looking for ways to connect service with broader social change.

The lessons and tools in this guide come directly from Raise Your Voice student leaders who have organized to give their peers more effective voices and power for addressing urgent public issues such as hunger, homelessness, educational reform, and the lack of young people in the political system. Included are a range of conceptual frameworks they developed, with new approaches to politics, community service, and higher education in support of student civic engagement. Also included are practical, user-friendly tools for effecting social change on campus and in the community.

The Problem: Disengaged Students and Campuses

In 1977, in an address at Douglass College, poet and activist Adrienne Rich declared: "The first thing I want to say to you who are students is that you cannot afford to think of being here to receive an education: you will do much better to think of being here to claim one."

After almost 30 years, the idea of claiming your education has become even more important as more colleges and universities treat students as passive consumers, rather than producers of their education. The student as customer is part of a broader societal trend. For example, students today report that "being well off financially" is far more important than "developing a meaningful philosophy of life," according to a recent survey of incoming college students conducted by the Higher Education Research Institute at UCLA (HERI, 2003). The survey shows that these goals have reversed during the past 40 years.

College students are by no means the me-focused youths often stereotyped in the media—they are, for example, volunteering in record numbers—but while they are giving freely of their time on an individual basis, they are less inclined to participate in civic or political affairs, at least as these activities are typically measured (see the sidebar on p. 3 for some statistics). Although HERI has found that students' political awareness has increased somewhat since its nadir in 2000, in 2003 still only a third of students said that "keeping up to date with political affairs" was very important. Every significant indicator of political engagement has fallen by at least half during the three decades in which the HERI has conducted its survey.

In many ways, higher education mirrors this disengagement with public issues. Colleges and universities are often seen as isolated bubbles that have little to do with local communities or broader public issues. They are organized as a series of quasi-independent boxes or silos that discourage collaboration, cooperation, or collegial action. As they become more privatized, they have less public support. Tuition at public and private colleges and universities continues to rise, and public funding for higher education continues to fall. In short, colleges and universities are often disengaged from solving the most important public problems, at a time when the public sees less need to support them.

The Solution: Organizing for Change

Many student leaders reject the notion of today's college students as "apathetic." More students are volunteering in communities now than in any previous generation. Many of these students combine service with activism; they are creating a new, more expansive, robust, and relational politics that is not measured by conventional indicators of engagement. They are talking about issues with their peers, buying socially responsible products, and demanding that large institutions (including their own colleges and universities) support their efforts to make the world a better place.

In the Raise Your Voice campaign during the past three years, student leaders have conducted asset-mapping projects on hundreds of campuses; led public dialogues on issues such as housing, child care, and the war in Iraq; engaged in campus strategic planning; met with their state legislators in more than a dozen states; and connected service and politics through projects such as alternative spring breaks to Washington, DC. Each example confirms that democracy is something best learned through the practical application of everyday politics and thoughtful strategic planning by being an active and reflective member of a community.

Student leaders are also helping to change the culture on campuses across the country. They are demanding that colleges and universities offer students the opportunity for democratic action through involvement in their community, support for political change, and opportunities to have a say in the curriculum. They are demanding to have a real voice, both on campus issues and on issues of broader impact.

The key question is this: *How can you influence a huge institution like a college or university to organize for democratic and social change?* We who have been a part of Raise Your Voice know that while students may not have powerful roles on all campuses, it is possible to influence organizations whose very longevity is testament to their resistance to change. We have a unique role to play on campus and in society. We can ask the difficult questions, experiment with innovative solutions, and bring fresh perspectives to divisive problems. Every campus is different, but if you are smart, strategic, and collaborative, you can develop an inclusive process that encourages the dialogue necessary for building long-term commitment. This guide offers many tools to help you get started.

> **Community Service and Politics: Statistics**
>
> - More than 75% of high school seniors reported volunteering in 2001, compared with 62% in 1976.
> - A majority (67%) of young people report volunteering at youth organizations, while only a handful (6%) volunteer for political organizations.
> - In 2004, 47% of 18- to 24-year-old citizens voted, up from 36% in 2000, but down substantially from 58% in 1972 when 18-year-olds first voted.*
>
> * Note that reported voting rates vary by source because of differences in how rates are calculated (e.g., rate of eligible as opposed to registered voters).
>
> SOURCE: The Center for Information & Research on Civic Learning & Engagement (CIRCLE). See www.civicyouth.org for detailed data analyses.

Using This Book

The guide is divided into four chapters and an appendix. In Chapter 1, students reflect on lessons learned through their experiences as civic engagement leaders with Raise Your Voice. They overwhelmingly point to the need for institutions to provide direct support—in the form of financial, physical, and mentoring resources—for students' efforts to engage their peers. Chapter 1 also offers key strategies for overcoming barriers to student engagement, as well as the conceptual and definitional grounding for a new student politics on campus.

The next three chapters contain practical applications for making change happen on your campus. These chapters will help you have an effective, powerful voice on campus and community issues by becoming an effective organizer and facilitator of change.

Raise Your Voice students have learned that in order for students to be effective agents of campus change, they must be *deliberate* and *strategic* by using a method called "community mapping," described in Chapter 2. The chapter has a guide for finding stakeholders, allies, and resources on campus and working collaboratively with these stakeholders on the issues you care most about.

Raise Your Voice students have also learned that effective organizing requires reflection and consensus building. Chapter 3 contains a step-by-step guide to facilitating dialogues, creating public forums and learning circles, and having deliberative conversations among peers, faculty, staff, and administrators. The guide has everything you need for implementing successful dialogues on campus, including examples of topics, formats, and facilitation and evaluation techniques, as well as sample dialogues.

As noted earlier, today's students are far from apathetic, but that they are more likely to perform direct service than other forms of civic engagement. Chapter 4 offers data, tools, and ideas for connecting direct service and the political system. It also has advice on becoming politically engaged and provides models for successfully connecting service and politics on campus.

The appendix offers a train-the-trainer guide for student leaders, campus staff and faculty, and community partners. This final section includes both sample trainings and agendas.

This guide is not meant to be read cover to cover. It is a resource with targeted information for students who want to change the world, starting with their own campus. As we pass on the lessons from our efforts to make change, we hope it will inspire creative, innovative activism on college campuses.

DICK CONE
ABBY KIESA
NICK LONGO

References

Higher Education Research Institute. (2003). *The American freshman: National norms for fall 2003.* Los Angeles: University of California.

Horton, M., & Freire, P. (1991). *We make the road by walking: Conversations on education and social change.* Philadelphia: Temple University Press.

Lessons Learned on the Road to Student Civic Engagement

In this student-written declaration on campus engagement, Raise Your Voice (RYV) student leaders Tara Germond (University of Rhode Island), Ellen Love (Brown University), Liz Moran (University of Illinois, Springfield), Sherita Moses (Langston University), and Stephanie Raill (Macalester College) provide a theoretical foundation for students making change on campus.[1] The document provides a conceptual framework for student activism and includes practical guidance and advice for getting started on your campus.

The story of how this document was written is compelling. Thirty student leaders from campuses around the United States spent a weekend in Chicago in June 2004, discussing the ideas and strategies they had used in their organizing efforts on campus. The conversation included stories, shared obstacles to civic engagement, and lessons for engaging other students. After the weekend retreat, the work of the five student authors began. Their goal was to write a statement that reflected the conversation in Chicago but that also took it to a deeper level. There was much information to draw on, including the experiences of the student authors themselves, along with notes, student interviews, and countless hours of conversations compiled over a two-year period.

The authors describe the strategies that RYV student leaders found most effective and important, and share what inspires students to action and what sometimes discourages them about political and community engagement. The declaration begins with an introduction to describe the context of the document and the Raise Your Voice campaign. The next sections examine barriers to engagement, best practices for overcoming those barriers, and the essential elements to consider in establishing student-centered civic engagement. The discussions that follow challenge institutions of higher education to make preparing active citizens a key priority and envision the

---

1. This declaration is available as a separate publication: *Lesson Learned on the Road to Student Civic Engagement* (Campus Compact, 2006).

engaged campus from a student perspective. The declaration ends with a call to action that includes strategies you can use to get started on your own campus.

RYV and Student Engagement

In 2001, Campus Compact—a national nonprofit association dedicated to fulfilling the civic purposes of higher education—convened the Wingspread Summit on Student Civic Engagement. At this gathering, student leaders from around the United States talked about their experiences with and perceptions of civic engagement and democracy, education, service, and politics. The summit led to two groundbreaking initiatives: the publication of *The New Student Politics: The Wingspread Statement on Student Civic Engagement* (Long, 2002), Campus Compact's first published student statement on civic engagement; and the beginning of the Raise Your Voice campaign, which eventually involved hundreds of thousands of students across the country.

Supported by a $2.8 million multiyear grant from The Pew Charitable Trusts and based on the insights of the Wingspread students, Campus Compact developed and initiated the RYV campaign with three distinct goals:

1. Increase college student involvement in public life and connect these actions with a larger national student movement on civic engagement.

2. Document student civic engagement activities and issues important to college students.

3. Mobilize higher education in a way that gives greater voice to students and makes civic engagement central to student learning.

With these goals, Campus Compact set out to use its national structure, which includes nearly 1,000 member campuses and 31 state offices, to connect hundreds of campus initiatives supported by Raise Your Voice. State Campus Compact offices hired coordinators in many states, who then used Campus Compact's extensive relationships with campuses—particularly with presidents and community service and service-learning directors—to identify students to be the campaign's leaders.

Based on the state's discretion, state coordinators used varying strategies to organize and train the campus leaders. In Oklahoma and Illinois, for example, state coordinators organized a student advisory board that meets regularly to collaborate on projects and direct the state's RYV campaign. Other states, such as Minnesota and Rhode Island, initiated competitive student fellowship programs that focused on training and developing student leaders to work on campus initiatives.

The national student campaign grew from just 33 Wingspread Summit students in 2001 to 270,000+ students on more than 500 campuses in 32 states between 2002 and 2005. The campaign's broad goals allowed student leaders to mold their activities to their campuses' engagement levels and interests. When students felt their peers were not talking about important issues, they instituted campus dialogues. When students were discussing issues, RYV leaders challenged them to actively participate through direct service or political action. On many campuses, students used a process of "mapping" resources, allies, and power dynamics to understand engagement more deeply. The nonpartisan movement to invite and encourage students to engage in the public sphere spread rapidly across the country, especially among students who felt that their participation had not previously been solicited or supported.

Three years later, the experience of RYV student leaders tells much about what students need and want in their education in order to become active, engaged community members and professionals. Their experience is one of growth in understanding the meaning and significance of "civic engagement" and how that term takes shape on a college campus.

This chapter describes how students faced the challenge of exploring the concept of civic engagement—what it means to them, how it looks on their campus, what kinds of activities they consider civically engaged—in their own words. It also describes how students came to realize that they alone could not create a sustainable culture of engagement on campuses. Institutions of higher education must make substantial changes if civic engagement is to become the norm for college students. We argue that civic engagement is an important part of higher learning and that civic learning is central to our education.

Our goals are: (1) to accurately reflect the voices of RYV leaders and pass on their lessons about how to engage students, and (2) to provide some insight about higher education as a whole. We start with a hands-on discussion of the barriers to engagement on campus and best practices for overcoming those barriers, including ways to collaborate, cut through bureaucracy, mobilize students, connect engaged activity with the curriculum, and sustain engagement efforts. Individual students and student groups will find practical advice for finding the right people and using the right tactics to create lasting change.

We then move to more theoretical territory, exploring what civic engagement means and what it looks like. While there is no broad consensus, even among RYV student leaders, about what "civic engagement" is or how a civically engaged person might behave, we provide an analysis of the term based on our experiences. We expand on the idea of service politics developed in *The New Student Politics* and explore the components of civic engagement and service-learning. At the end of this discussion, we provide a working definition of civic engagement so students can join and expand on the conversation.

Next we explore the role of higher education in fostering civic engagement, including preparing students for all aspects of public life. Finally, we lay out a vision of the engaged campus based on the strategies, best practices, and definitions explored in the earlier sections. This discussion offers a range of ideas for how and where to begin the long process of building an active, civically engaged campus.

Our hope is that these lessons inspire institutions of higher education to fulfill their role as places where citizens can freely find, train, and raise their individual and collective voices in our great but fragile democracy.

Barriers and Best Practices

Students in the Raise Your Voice campaign have learned valuable lessons about campus cultures, institutional structures, and the tools needed to best engage their peers. Accounts of student work from across the nation identified specific challenges students faced and effective strategies they used to promote civic engagement on their campuses. While these challenges and strategies were as varied as the hundreds of campuses involved, some common themes emerged.

The strategies that RYV student leaders used often attempted to overcome or circumvent difficult barriers to organizing on college campuses. RYV leaders worked systematically to develop strategies to meet the specific challenges on their campuses. Some were highly successful and will strengthen future attempts to increase civic engagement on college campuses. Other responses were stopgap measures that show us where more institutional support for civic engagement is necessary.

These practical strategies—the heart of the RYV campaign—are useful for anyone working to involve college students in democratic action. The detailed observations and best practices for getting students involved are what led students to the broader conclusions about the role of higher education in the sections that follow.

1. Networking and Collaboration

ISSUE—FRAGMENTED CAMPUSES

Raise Your Voice students identified collaboration and networking as essential tools for overcoming the complex physical and social fragmentation of many higher education institutions. When asked about obstacles they faced, students in Chicago commonly responded that campuses are disconnected. Many observed that student organizations do not work with each other, campuses are not involved with local communities, and complex bureaucracies can prevent students from working with administrations.

This problem is twofold. First, lack of coordination among campus civic engagement programs limits the resources that support action for change, which in turn limits how many students can become involved. One RYV student leader found that every spring two different departmental programs at his university hosted nearly identical events for underprivileged youth to visit the campus. Neither organization knew the other program existed. If these groups had collaborated, they could have used their resources to do more advertising and recruiting, thus engaging a larger group of students.

Second, the fragmentation of civic engagement programs limits the scope and energy of activities, which in turn results in fewer students being inspired to join. Susan Sayball, a student from Mount Wachusett Community College in Massachusetts, was one of many RYV participants who recognized that student engagement efforts often do not realize their full potential: "Clubs and organizations try to do their own thing; they forget that they can become a stronger circle if they come together with other groups to do a big thing versus a bunch of small things."

STRATEGY—COLLABORATE ACROSS STUDENT GROUPS AND DEPARTMENTS
It is valuable for students to have many avenues that lead to engagement—a service-learning class, a Caribbean heritage club, a political party, or an environmental organization. Students should be able to find types of engagement that fit their personal or academic interests. While not always necessary, collaboration is likely to strengthen civic engagement projects. Collaboration may manifest itself solely through regular communication or it may take the form of joint programs. Either way, a unified effort is often more powerful than the sum of its parts.

Students utilized collaboration and relational networking as a way to bridge the gaps between disconnected communities of students and other individuals. In response to social and administrative fragmentation of opportunities for action, many RYV students chose to assume the role of connector, bridging the gaps between different constituencies on campus. They researched the activities of pre-established organizations and, rather than create a new student group, worked to connect already existing groups. By connecting these groups, RYV student leaders built unified collective action that inspired and drew a wide range of students. The energy and excitement of large, collaborative actions is much more likely to attract disengaged students (or motivate marginally engaged ones).

The flexibility of the Raise Your Voice campaign made it a strong vehicle for connecting various constituents and mobilizing strong coalitions. RYV student leaders were not bound to any particular issue; they took ownership of their work and addressed the most important concerns on their campuses. Although some RYV staff found that the breadth of the campaign made it hard to summarize for administrators or prospective participants, the flexible structure lent itself to building coalitions. Students, staff, and faculty were willing to work with a non-partisan group that had not already been boxed in to one particular area of campus.

As Eliana Machuca, a student from Humboldt State University, pointed out, "I think that RYV came at one of the most appropriate times because there is, or was, this underlying buzz where student organizations wanted to communicate with each other.... I think that it has started...all of us in the Community Service Center planting these seeds of student collaboration and bringing groups together to work on things." Machuca called herself a "spider woman" for the way she, like other RYV students, wove webs among the many different, fragmented communities of students and student organizations on her campus.

2. Connecting Institutions and Their Communities

ISSUE—DISCONNECT BETWEEN CAMPUS AND COMMUNITY

At many colleges, there is a disconnect between the campus and its surroundings. Social and physical barriers often separate students from the rest of the local community. At many four-year institutions, students come from a wide geographic area and are unfamiliar with the school's locale. They feel little responsibility to the community and have no knowledge of how to become involved off campus. Longtime residents of the surrounding area may also be wary of students and their possible impact. When there are no formal connections between the campus and the outside community, students have difficulty engaging in action for change off campus, which decreases the potential for the formation of community-campus partnerships.

STRATEGY—BUILD COLLABORATIVE PARTNERSHIPS

Raise Your Voice leaders reacted to this disconnect by providing information about the local community to students. For example, RYV Fellow Amy Fitzgerald and other RYV students at the Rhode Island School of Design built an online database of volunteer opportunities that are available to students through local agencies. By creating a database, Fitzgerald formed relationships with dozens of community organizations and provided an easy resource to help students become engaged with their local community.

RYV students also established reciprocal partnerships between on-campus groups and off-campus community groups. When these partnerships are truly reciprocal, they are both effective and mutually beneficial. For example, when architecture students at the Rhode Island School of Design helped Habitat for Humanity build a house, they not only hammered nails and carried boards but also helped read the blueprints for the project and discussed architectural design with the contractor. They returned from the event having worked with a family on their new home, excited to have used their skills and prepared to bring their friends next time.

Community groups can give students invaluable learning experiences. Volunteers at service organizations, interns at government agencies, or assistants in nonprofit groups provide valuable labor, but they also learn a lot about society, government, social change, and citizenship. For example, RYV students at Humboldt State University in California collaborated with a local group at Arcata High School to organize a town hall meeting about local referendum issues in the 2004 election. Students often report that such community collaborations are among the most powerful of their college career.

Finally, some RYV leaders assessed the relationship between their college or university and the community and worked to improve it. By pressuring their institutions to demonstrate a sincere commitment to their local community, the leaders built the foundation for future collaboration. For example, one student examined labor relations on her campus. Disappointed by the lack of commitment shown by her peers and administrators to campus employees, she took the initiative to establish a language exchange program between employees and students. The language exchange is a good example of a reciprocal relationship in which both parties benefit. The students are a contributing part of the surrounding community, and the employees build necessary language skills to use on campus and in other areas of life.

3. Navigating Complex Bureaucracies
ISSUE—ADMINISTRATIVE PROTOCOLS
A common refrain among RYV student leaders was that college bureaucracies are difficult to navigate. Some RYV students found that the structures of their administrative offices hindered student action; they had to learn to wade through complex structures or work without much administrative support. Even when a number of service-learning or community service staff people support student voice and leadership (which was the case on most RYV campuses), it often took students many months to learn the correct avenues for working with higher-level administrators. Often it was a combination of the structural and procedural fragmentation that acted as a barrier; students might need to fill out a form in the student affairs office in the administrative building, but process it through the student activities office in the student union. Or maybe they have to seek out the dean of the college to get permission to use a room.

Regina Whitedirt of Chief Dull Knife College in Montana described the steps it takes to establish a relationship with the administration at most colleges as "protocol." The problem, she noted, is not that protocol exists but that it is often complex and opaque. New students don't know where to go with plans for an environmental residence hall, a support group for international students, or other ideas. Students are usually on campus for only four years, and by the time they learn the ropes of the institution, they are ready to don a cap and gown.

Students need administrative support to organize events on campus and get their peers to take action, but the complex, fragmented structure of campus bureaucracies sometimes prevents them from accessing needed resources. As campus leaders, administrators are extremely busy. In most cases, however, it is their support and commitment that students most need.

STRATEGY—CREATE CAMPUS MAPS
Many Raise Your Voice students created detailed campus "maps" as a way to identify potential allies on campus, available resources, organizational structures, and areas where gaps exist on campus. Through mapping, students gained a broader understanding of their institution, helping them to become more efficient and knowledgeable when trying to effect change. Mapping allows students to develop strategies for action, form relationships that will strengthen efforts, and find additional resources to promote student involvement.

Many RYV students used the Mapping Resource Guide that RYV staff created for students (see Chapter 2). Emily Yee, for example, found that the mapping tool helped her to organize at University of California at San Diego. Because her campus has six separate colleges, she initially found it difficult to locate administrators who could help her organize events and recruit students across them all. She, like hundreds of other students, found the mapping effort invaluable in helping her see the overall structure of her campus and use existing allies and resources.

A one-time mapping project is helpful in the short term, but it is not a good way to create sustained student action. Unless student leaders deliberately pass on their knowledge of campus bureaucracies, the next group of incoming students will have to learn the system all over again. The best mapping projects include strategies to make the information available to incoming students or upcoming leaders in a student organization as well as a process to update the information on a continuing basis.

4. Engaging the Disengaged

ISSUE—ISOLATED AND DETACHED LIVES
In addition to structural and administrative barriers, broad societal cynicism and detachment encourage disengagement. Although many students and young adults

do community service and a larger percentage of young adults voted in 2004 than in the previous four elections, millions of students are still completely detached from civic life (CIRCLE, 2004).

Nonetheless, students who are not civically engaged should not simply be characterized as lazy or apathetic. Many complex factors underlie some students' tendency to disengage from community work or politics. They may distrust public figures, they may work full time to support their studies, they may have children who demand their time, or they simply may not believe that one person's contribution will make a difference. Barriers to engagement include not just video games, television, and the Thursday to Sunday party scene, but also important responsibilities such as jobs, coursework, athletics, and families.

STRATEGY—USE RELATIONAL ORGANIZING

Students at the Lessons Learned gathering spoke overwhelmingly of the need to use personal relationships in their efforts to engage their peers. This "relational organizing" can make student-led engagement unique and powerful. Students alone don't have the ability to penalize their peers for lack of engagement through the grading system or to offer academic credit for participation, although many collaborate with faculty and staff to leverage these tools. What they do have is access to their classmates on a personal and social level. Students use social networks to bring people to the table, with strategies such as personal phone calls and social events, for both recruitment and retention.

As Summer Stowe-Johnson of Oklahoma State University explained, "All of us have been asked to do this. And it had to be personal—someone saying, 'We want you to do this.'" With so many ways to spend time, personal connections are often what make the difference between spending Monday afternoon playing video games and mentoring an elementary school student. Figuring out how each student can become involved depends on creating varied entry points for students to get involved based on their own responsibilities and interests.

Relational organizing is particularly important for motivating students to become active in electoral politics. Rather than focusing on issues that media outlets or politicians deem important, RYV students often concentrated on issues that were closer to home, such as education funding cuts, tuition increases, and inflated textbook prices. By appealing to students' personal lives, RYV students could overcome a sense of distance and detachment from politics.

This strategy takes a great deal of time, but its impact can be extensive. A few students, once engaged, can recruit an ever-widening circle of peers. We have learned that relational organizing is important not only for engaging others but also for helping students value the process of building lasting relationships and developing the skills needed to do so.

5. Finding Our Allies

ISSUE—LACK OF FINANCIAL SUPPORT FOR CIVIC ENGAGEMENT
Many students and student organizations do not have the offices, resources, or support to be effective on campus. Without funding for making photocopies, renting microphones, and all the other expenses of running a program, their impact is limited. Although inadequate support was a major barrier for students trying to plan events and programs, RYV student leaders discovered that they had allies on campus who could assist them in their efforts.

STRATEGY—COLLABORATE TO SAVE RESOURCES
RYV students often worked out of the campus community service or service-learning office. Staff from these offices frequently acted as advisers, helping students with organization and administrative details and guiding them through the complex institutional structure.

Students saved energy and time by partnering with campus staff who had additional knowledge about their institution's structure and operations. Forming supportive relationships with these individuals helped students develop a better understanding of protocol and gave them the guidance they needed to sustain their morale and motivation to continue their work. Many attendees at the Chicago conference cited their institution's community service directors, advisers, and other supportive staff as central to their success.

6. Sustaining Engagement

ISSUE—NEED FOR DEEPENING ENGAGEMENT
Miscellaneous events that engage people for half an hour on a Wednesday night are not enough to create a genuinely engaged atmosphere in a campus community. "After two years working on the Raise Your Voice campaign, we must recognize that we cannot depend on the exciting and romantic notion that real commitment to civic engagement will grow from throwing students together in momentary activities," explains Dick Cone of California Campus Compact. Individual events are valuable in connecting people and regularly produce positive results with the participants, but lasting civic engagement comes only from longer projects and ongoing conversations.

STRATEGY—CONNECT EVENTS TO LARGER ISSUES
Students who created lasting impact and significant progress in the civic engagement movement took strategic action by moving away from planning disconnected events and toward understanding how these events fit into a broader scheme.

Events connected to a larger issue help to put the event in context, such as how the loss of employment in a depleting economy leads to homelessness, or how U.S. economic policies may affect hunger in less developed countries. These connections help participants understand their roles in creating change.

The RYV students who focused on long-term projects achieved significant, lasting results. Jacole Douglas and her co-leaders at the University of Montana instituted an ethics pledge for their campus. Students in Vermont organized a student government body nearly from scratch. Students at Carroll College in Montana organized a sustainable after-school program for children in a transitional housing center. Many other examples from the RYV campaign highlight what can be achieved when students move beyond one-time events and make long-term commitments to their projects. In doing so, students learned what it takes to be strategic and rally others around a long-term vision.

7. Understanding the Importance of Diversity

ISSUE—LACK OF DIVERSITY IN STUDENT ENGAGEMENT EFFORTS

To be effective at promoting civic engagement on campus, students have to reach out to a diversity of people, departments, and organizations—one of the greatest challenges for RYV students. Identifying RYV student leaders, on most campuses, was facilitated by an existing infrastructure of relationships with Campus Compact, mainly through community service and service-learning offices. Although this broad infrastructure, which connects many different people on campus, is one of Campus Compact's strengths, the people that it connects do not typically represent the full diversity of a campus. Statistics show that women comprise the majority of campus service participants and that most campus service programs involve students who are in the ethnic and racial majority. (See, for example, *Campus Compact's 2001 Annual Survey Statistics,* available at www.compact.org/news/stats2001/survey3.html.)

As evidence of a larger tension within campus engagement, on most campuses the people who care deeply about issues of diversity—specifically concerning race, class, and gender—often cluster in multicultural centers, women's and ethnic studies departments, or identity-based fraternities and sororities rather than community service or service-learning offices. Only a handful of students addressed these issues through Raise Your Voice, although some RYV state staff, recognizing that lack of diversity limited the potential of the movement, were able to develop sustained relationships to work outside of community service offices.

STRATEGY—INVOLVE A WIDE VARIETY OF GROUPS

A diverse civic engagement movement can influence a broader range of campus constituents and student interests. One RYV student worked to bring diverse groups of students and student organizations on her campus together for a program focused on educating others about discrimination and modern oppression. She saw that the multicultural groups on her campus were not working with each other or with other student organizations, so she developed a diversity education program to bring these different groups and different voices together. Through this program, many students and groups were able to work with, learn from, and form relationships with each other.

To establish a broad, strong movement focused on civic engagement, students must build relationships outside of the spheres of community service and student life and work with the diversity movement on campuses, along with student organizations, multicultural groups, faculty, staff, and the community. Forming partnerships with these constituents will help to expand reach on campus and ensure that the voices represented in the movement are as diverse as possible.

8. Connecting with the Curriculum

ISSUE—CLASSROOM DYNAMICS

As the campaign progressed, RYV student leaders realized that they could reach many more students if they could tie civic engagement to interesting academic work. Unfortunately, the power dynamics of classrooms usually inhibit suggestions from students about teaching and learning. It was not easy for RYV students to ask professors to incorporate service-learning and civic education into their courses. Therefore, finding ways to reach unengaged students through classrooms was often a major challenge.

STRATEGY—APPROACH INTERESTED FACULTY

Classrooms are a significant part of higher education, and when professors incorporate civic engagement into the curriculum, they engage many students that student leaders cannot reach alone. Professors can assign students service requirements or another civic engagement activity as part of the class, or they can teach the knowledge and skills that will help students be active community members later in life. Both of these techniques foster engagement on campus, and ideally both would occur simultaneously across the curriculum to engage students in every department.

While it is difficult for students to initiate civic and service-learning on campus, students can work with professors who already use service-learning or teach civic skills. The vast majority of RYV students organized co-curricular (non-classroom–related) activities, but a few RYV students approached professors who already encouraged civic engagement and asked them to collaborate on an RYV project.

For example, two RYV leaders found that service-learning professors were amenable to hosting in-class dialogues about public issues. Summer Stowe-Johnson talked with a professor who was trying to establish one of the first service-learning classes on campus. Since the professor was already trying to engage students, Stowe-Johnson felt comfortable asking the professor to host a dialogue between students and local veterans to educate students about recent wars and veterans' issues. A student in California leveraged a service-learning course to host a dialogue in class. The topic was politically charged, and students appreciated the safe, nonpartisan classroom environment in which to talk. Both activities involved students who might never have attended a co-curricular event but who valued the dialogue skills and knowledge they gained through classroom-based civic learning.

When professors show their students how to use what they are learning and how it is relevant to society, they foster engaged learners. When classrooms become central spaces for engagement, with the incorporation of more service and civic learning, a partnership based on equality and reciprocity is more likely to prevail among all stakeholders in institutions, including the local community.

9. Encouraging Political Engagement

ISSUE—STUDENTS' ALIENATION FROM POLITICS

Statistics show that 18- to 24-year-olds participate in electoral politics at lower than average rates. They are less likely to vote, sign petitions, or participate in electoral campaigns than are those in older age groups. Statistics on college students indicate that they often participate in service and other types of community work and tend to shy away from traditional politics. (See "Summary of Student Surveys," in Long, 2002, pp. 22–24.) RYV leaders found planning political events difficult because many students did not want to be linked to the word *politics,* nor did they trust politicians.

STRATEGY—CONNECT CIVIC AND COMMUNITY ENGAGEMENT

We found that in general, few RYV students initially chose projects that connected with legislators and elected officials. Because of their mistrust of electoral politics and because approaching elected officials can be intimidating, students usually chose other avenues of engagement. When RYV staff organized meetings with legislators and elected officials, students were enthusiastic and often took the lead in organizing subsequent meetings with policymakers.

Two of the most successful ways to connect students to traditional politics were Days at the State House and alternative spring break trips. Fifteen RYV states held Days at the State House or other programs that connected students and elected officials. These events, typically organized statewide, involved students from many different colleges converging at the state capitol to meet with their legislators. At some events, students lobbied legislators about a particular issue, while at others, students participated in general question-and-answer sessions with their representatives. The goal was to familiarize students with the political process and to let elected officials know that students care about a variety of issues that affect them.

Alternative spring break trips made politics relevant to students by including both political and service components. Maine Campus Compact, for example, organized a trip to Washington, DC, with the theme of hunger and homelessness. During their spring break in 2003, a group of students from several Maine campuses volunteered at a homeless shelter, discussed hunger and homelessness with advocacy groups in Washington, and finally met with their legislators to promote legislation aimed at reducing hunger and homelessness in the United States. The trip was successful in educating and energizing students about the specific issue, and it also empowered them to try to get to the root causes of community issues by working within the political system.

The students who participated in state house days or alternative breaks were able to talk about legislation and show their elected officials that they were serious. Students spoke with many representatives, senators, and governors to convince them that young people are not apathetic, and that students will respond if public officials reach out to them. In most cases, both groups left the events understanding that the other group has a role to play, and that each group should be conscious of the other's roles and expectations.

In addition, when students addressed legislation on issues, they were able to see the connection between those issues and other policies and political processes that affect them. Amanda Coffin of the University of Maine at Farmington noted: "I have always had a drive to serve others and work for the common good. But I never fully realized that I could go beyond volunteerism, that my opinion and hard work could influence policy decisions. My views changed when I sat in the office of one of my legislators in Washington, DC, as part of a group of Maine students on an alternative break trip." Coffin is like many students who just need to understand the connection between policy and their own lives.

10. Creating Space for Student Voice

ISSUE—NEED FOR STUDENTS TO BE HEARD
Deliberative, open dialogue is a central part of the democratic process. Even schools that have extensive civic engagement programs are often less rigorous in teaching students to develop and utilize their civic voice.

For those who want to promote student voice in campus decision making, the culture of passivity and the ingrained mistrust of student voice are often difficult to overcome. Silence, RYV students found, is usually linked to fear of embarrassment and a lack of skills and confidence. It was not easy for students to win the trust of administrators and build substantial avenues for student voice, although a few found ways to do so.

One barrier is that administrators often make decisions that affect students and their civic engagement without student input. Fearing that students will make rash, uninformed decisions, many institutions hesitate to incorporate their voices in institutional decision-making processes. At many schools students are not present at decision-making tables at all, while at others an isolated student sits on one or more administrative committees. Although student governments offer some voice, many view the power granted through student government to be a token gesture.

STRATEGY—PRACTICE DEVELOPING VOICE

Students discovered that the best strategy for overcoming this dynamic was to create spaces on campus to find and practice using their voice. The knowledge to formulate opinions, the confidence to articulate points, and the skill to listen to others' views do not come naturally. It is important to learn ways of speaking and of listening that promote understanding and encourage action. Hundreds of RYV students organized dialogues on their campuses. The goal was to engage their peers in respectful, deliberate conversations about important issues, ranging from alcohol consumption to gay marriage. The common thread was the student facilitators' commitment to ensuring that each participant could speak and be heard.

Most participants at the Chicago conference agreed that that RYV's nonpartisan stance was critical to hosting successful dialogues. They noted that if RYV had been partisan, it would have been unable to draw unengaged or loosely engaged students to community dialogues. Students also found that participants must be on an equal footing with everyone in the room. Having peer moderators rather than experts was one way that students tried to make the dialogues safe, democratic spaces. Telling personal stories to make students comfortable with talking in front of a group was another useful strategy.

A few students overcame administrative reluctance to trust student voice and built permanent avenues for bringing their opinions to their administrations, especially when they could find allies or could argue that student voice would make programs run more smoothly. For example, at Princeton, James Williams was part of an umbrella group of students and administrators who served as equals in addressing the needs of all the different service or civic engagement programs on campus. According to Williams, student voice is critical on the committee because students have a better cross-departmental view than many administrators.

Greater student voice in campus affairs can help students build their confidence to speak up in other areas. In the few places where students gained a sustained voice in campus affairs, they not only felt more connected to their schools, they were also able to offer a valuable new perspective. Student representation can give administrators valuable insights into students' views on a given policy, reactions to new decisions, and ideas that excite or inspire them.

Nearly all the RYV students concurred that training was one of the best pieces of the RYV program. Most of the student leaders received training in moderating respectful, comfortable dialogues and were able to create open space for dialogue on their campuses.

Civic Engagement—A Definition Through Action

The breadth of the RYV campaign was one of its greatest strengths. However, the diversity of approaches to civic engagement on different campuses and the relative lack of contact among students from different states meant that when we came together to share lessons, we had trouble communicating because we lacked a shared vocabulary that could describe all our experiences. Our goal here is to prompt more conversation and provide a framework for developing this vocabulary. We do not intend to represent a consensus; this is based on our analyses and observations from the conversations in Chicago about students' own experiences with service, politics, and civic engagement.

A New Understanding of Student Engagement

The book that catalyzed the Raise Your Voice campaign, *The New Student Politics*, suggested that student civic engagement could be classified into three distinct categories:

- Service—conventional community service or volunteerism
- Politics—participating in electoral or governmental political processes such as voting or writing to legislators
- Service politics—using service-like activities to work toward broader change

According to *The New Student Politics,* as students become more engaged, they naturally move from doing service alone to engaging in a mixture of politics and service, which is a more effective tool for social change. The book was a vital step toward giving voice to students' own understanding of their civic engagement work. It did not represent the opinions of all students, or all student leaders, but it catalyzed discussion among student leaders and service-learning professionals.

Many Raise Your Voice leaders were introduced to the definition of service politics as they began work on the campaign. Some agreed with it because it gave a platform to students who argued that their service work was political; others came to the campaign from backgrounds of volunteerism or political activism and saw their favored strategy as the most effective means of achieving social change. Throughout the campaign, we gained a more nuanced understanding of students' descriptions of civic engagement, and when and how it is most effective.

We learned that what is important is not whether you are engaged in service or in politics. Indeed, there are methods of engagement outside these two categories; for example, living as though the decisions you make in your life will affect others is a form of engagement. What is important is that you are truly engaged: you know what part your work plays in a larger movement toward social change. However, as we learned, the more engaged you are, the more likely it is that you will use a variety of tactics to achieve your goals.

Reframing the Dialogue

FROM SERVICE TO SOCIAL ENGAGEMENT

Although community service was an important part of students' work in the Raise Your Voice campaign, it does not adequately describe all activities that do not fit neatly into the category of *politics*. When people hear the word *service*, they tend to think of volunteering; images of soup kitchens and homeless shelters spring to mind. But the array of activities students led and took part in extends much farther. Activities varied from power mapping to working with communities to identify their assets to facilitating on-campus dialogues to designing and executing experiential learning activities for understanding oppression. It is clear that students' desire to affect their communities directly is not limited to spending two hours a week with a ladle at the ready.

To better describe the range of strategies employed by students, we suggest using the term *social engagement* to describe the social or community-oriented strategies students employ to create change.

WHAT DO WE MEAN BY POLITICS?

Say the word *politics* to a group of students—even a group of Raise Your Voice leaders—and you will likely hear back *corrupt, irrelevant*, and *full of old, rich white men*. Even students active in politics have had many negative associations and experiences in the political realm. These associations make the word politics troublesome. In addition, politics means different things to different people. Most students said that the word made them think of activities related to government and the electoral process, such as voting, lobbying, protesting, or running for office. Only a few used it to refer to other actions that reflect one's political convictions (for example, buying fair-trade bananas because of concern for the work conditions of the growers).

We suggest using the term *political engagement* to describe the strategies students use within the political system to create change, and *social engagement* to describe the intersection of political engagement and community service. *Political engagement* is a much less loaded term than *politics*, emphasizing political actions taken in order to create positive change.

A THIRD DIMENSION? ECONOMIC ENGAGEMENT

Does the sociopolitical spectrum adequately describe all possible forms of engagement? In endeavoring to answer this question, we were drawn to the example of Brian Abernathy, a student at Metro State University in Minnesota. As the University Student Activity Budget Liaison, he distributed money to student organizations. He also worked with organizations to encourage collaboration, not only because it would lead to better, more rewarding events but also because it would keep costs down and allow funds to stretch farther. As a result of his work, exploring opportunities for collaboration is now required for organizations seeking funding.

Abernathy's work was certainly engaged, and it led to positive change on his campus. But it doesn't fit neatly into the category of either service or politics. It could be described as *economic engagement*—using economic strategies to create social change. Students in Chicago spoke about other tactics of economic engagement. Many cited examples of being engaged consumers; they choose to buy organic produce or shop at local businesses because they realize that the impact of their spending extends beyond value for money.

MULTIFACETED ISSUES REQUIRE MULTIPLE TACTICS

Social engagement and political engagement should not be seen as discrete categories into which all activities can be easily classified. They represent two points on a spectrum. Activities that have both social and political dimensions fit somewhere between volunteerism and involvement with government. An example could be organizing a fundraising event for a homeless shelter, inviting politicians to attend, and asking them to consider changes to housing policy. Such an activity generates a social benefit—more resources for the shelter—and promotes policy change to address the underlying issue.

Rarely is an issue faced by a community purely social, political, or economic; most issues have aspects of all three. Homelessness, for example, is a social problem because the basic needs of community members are not being met. It is also an economic problem because of the resources used, for example, to provide emergency health care for an acute illness that could have been managed with medicine or a routine doctor's visit that a homeless person couldn't afford. It is a political problem because issues of public housing, zoning laws, and so on affect homelessness. Thus, to address homelessness effectively, we need to use social, economic, and political tactics. RYV students recognize this when they speak about the need for collaboration among diverse groups.

DEEP ENGAGEMENT AT THE INTERSECTIONS

Most RYV students believe that it makes sense to focus your energies on the area in which your skills will be most effective. Justin Horton, a student at Southern Illinois University Edwardsville, said, "I now understand that politics is important, but I'm just better at service, so that's what I choose to do." Not everybody has the confidence to approach a legislator to argue his or her point of view; not everybody enjoys the sometimes frustrating, messy work of hands-on service. We should be able to balance challenging ourselves and doing what we are good at.

It is important for students to be conscious of coordinating the employment of a range of strategies, but this balance does not need to be part of each student's individual work. It may manifest itself, as suggested earlier, in stronger partnerships among student organizations. It is true that more political engagement is needed for students to be an effective force for social change, but this should not be at the expense of the valuable social tactics to which they are committed.

We found that the more engaged students become, the more they find themselves using a wide variety of tactics to achieve their objectives. Many of the participants at the Chicago conference came from a background of community service; they noted a new understanding of the importance of political engagement as a result of the campaign. As Danica Willis of Saginaw Valley State University in Michigan explained, "We need to make real change through politics, doing something about the issues we observe through service." But just as numerous were the students who came from a political perspective and described their newfound desire to work in the social sector before, or as a complement to, fulfilling their political aspirations. They acknowledged that political change does not in itself change culture; as one said, "There are other ways to alleviate racial tension than passing a law."

Angelina Hamilton, a student leader at Eastern Michigan University (EMU), for example, delayed her matriculation at law school in order to take a VISTA position that will allow her to address the issues she cares about in a different way. As Hamilton stated,

> I had my whole life set out. I was going to graduate, then go to law school. In December 2002, I found out that I was pregnant. I was most stressed out because I still wanted to be involved in community service and everything that I was doing and I still wanted to go to law school. Then the baby was born and I realized I didn't have to stop everything, because I had a strong support . . . from

Michigan Campus Compact, my friends, my administrators, my bosses. So I was still able to do everything I wanted to do. It's led me to take a position as a VISTA [Volunteer in Service to America].... I could have taken a job with the government. But it was important to me to do a job that would make a difference, so I'm going to be a staff member at EMU working as a VISTA.

Engagement, then, is based on objectives rather than tactics. Focusing on the solution to the problem rather than on a particular method of addressing it leads to the use of a broader range of tactics encompassing all dimensions of engagement. The historical dimension of social change work does not elude us. Overwhelmingly, Raise Your Voice students acknowledged the need for social, political, and economic action in order to create real, sustainable change. Some choose to focus their actions solely or primarily in a specific sector because that is where they believe their skills and abilities are best used. But they recognize the necessity of coordinated, collaborative engagement in the social, political, and economic sectors to create systemic changes to benefit their communities.

Elements of Effective Student Engagement

ACTIVITY VS. ENGAGEMENT

So far, we have explored the three dimensions of engagement: social, political, and economic. But what is the difference between engagement and mere activity? To answer this question, we returned to students' discussions of civic engagement. They told us how they defined engagement, and how their definitions had changed over time. Students talked about the need to be informed, to see the bigger picture, to connect their work to deeper issues, and to learn from their experiences in order to be more effective next time.

Engagement is not a consequence of what sector you choose to work in, or what tactics you choose to create social change. No specific activities are inherently "engaged." Rather, it is the intention behind the activity that is important. Even the act of voting is not necessarily engaged. A vote cast purely by rote, because of coercion from friends or family, or to fulfill a legal obligation (in countries where it is compulsory to vote) *is not a civically engaged vote*. We are fulfilling our civic duty, but we are not civically engaged. However, when we have become informed about and considered the impact of our vote on our communities, then voting is civically engaged. The actual vote may (or may not) be the same, but the reason for voting is different. Likewise, volunteer work may be either engaged or unengaged (when it is compulsory or punitive, for example, although in such cases it may lead to engagement down the road).

Through RYV, we came to understand that three elements are essential to achieving the kind of civic engagement we believe is necessary for successful, sustained societal change: voice, action for change, and reflection. Engaged individuals include each of these elements in their efforts to create societal change.

VOICE

Voice was the quiet revolution the Raise Your Voice campaign brought to campuses. It gave students the skills to lead dialogues with their peers and connect students with people in power, such as legislators and administrators, who were able to act on their concerns and recommendations. "Raise Your Voice" started as a catchy name for the campaign, but the concept of voice resonated so powerfully among college students that we have tried to uncover what *voice* is and how it acts as an effective element of social change.

To exercise voice is to express ideas or opinions in a way that promotes understanding and/or change within a community or institution. Learning to raise our voices helps us to reject the resignation and powerlessness many students feel. We can use voice to strengthen a community through dialogue and mutual understanding, or to speak truth to power through protest and lobbying.

Effective voice has several essential elements:

- Inclusiveness—All stakeholders or community members should be encouraged and assisted in using their voice.

- A variety of perspectives—Questions and dissent should be welcomed as a process that leads to greater understanding and helps prevent irrelevant or destructive actions.

- Active listening—Voice includes both listening and being heard. Using your voice implies openness to listening to and being changed by others' voices.

Why is voice important for civic engagement? Voice is the basis of a democratic society. We need to know how to state opinions and effect change. We are in danger of becoming passive observers and consumers of the democratic process. Unless we learn how to voice our opinions and ideas, we will either fail to participate in the democracy or choose among candidates the way we choose among brands of peanut butter or sneakers. If we don't learn to raise our voices, we cede political influence to the groups who do.

In academia, we have an ideal forum in which to build confidence in using our voice and to discuss difficult issues that mainstream society avoids. Discussions of race, gender, religion, and class have been sidelined from mainstream discussions because people are afraid of making others uncomfortable. Major political parties are loathe to alienate swing voters. Even at family dinners, most of us restrain ourselves to avoid creating conflict.

But higher education is a venue in which we are supposed to learn new concepts, to reconcile others' ideas with our own, and to deepen our understanding of complex issues. We need to be careful that students who ask difficult questions of authority figures on campus or in the political world, or express opinions that do not reflect the status quo, do not find themselves silenced or marginalized through strategies like "free speech zones." This environment of learning and dialogue is an ideal place to have the discussions that we would sidestep elsewhere. Having this privilege has helped us realize how essential voice is for civic engagement.

ACTION FOR CHANGE

Action for change means acting in a way that creates a desired change within a community or institution. Students in the Raise Your Voice campaign organized and participated in many different kinds of action. Our skills in action were less developed than our skills in voice. Extensive work in building dialogue skills and learning to speak effectively about our concerns to allies and people in power has helped us realize the importance of making our actions more than a series of events if we are to achieve the kind of change we desire.

Essential elements of effective action are:

- Cohesiveness—Action must be sustained and strategic; individual actions should be connected with other actions around a common objective. The first lunch-counter sit-in did not make major civil rights changes; it took many sit-ins in many different places over time to achieve success. Likewise, for student action to be successful, it must be well-planned and executed, using skills of collaboration to draw together many people to work toward a goal.

- Effective groundwork—Action must be informed by the use of voice and information gathering. Speaking with and listening to others can help decide on a course of action, attract allies in positions of power, or show what action must be taken to influence powerful people because our voices have not been enough. If we do not first use voice, we risk alienating people who might have been willing to collaborate.

REFLECTION

To undertake reflection is to consider the extent to which our actions have been effective in achieving social change, and whether our actions are true to our values. Reflection is about learning from your actions and understanding your own beliefs, values, and needs so that you can share them with others by raising your voice and work toward meeting them through action for change.

Essential elements of reflection include:

- Self- and group evaluation—All civic engagement initiatives should include opportunities for individual and group reflection on the process and its outcomes, in addition to gathering numbers and statistics. Individual reflection helps us to understand how we have acted on our own goals, our individual and collective values, and our role in the success (or failure) of an initiative; group reflection helps us understand the lessons to be learned from an initiative as a whole.

- Critical examination of strengths and weaknesses—Reflection is often viewed as New Age mumbo-jumbo, too "touchy-feely" to be included in important initiatives. But reflection isn't about holding hands and telling ourselves how great we are. Reflection should involve honest, critical analysis of the strengths and weaknesses of the actions that have been taken. Ideally, reflection should lead a group to its next steps, whether to more effective use of voice or to a next set of actions.

What Is Civic Engagement? A Working Definition from a Student Perspective

There is certainly no consensus on a single definition of civic engagement. Nevertheless, as a result of the insights discussed above, we propose a definition here, both to serve as a talking point and to help clarify the meaning of this term as it is used in this document.

Engagement is more than just volunteering, although volunteering can be engagement. Engagement is more than just voting, although voting can be engagement. Engagement is a combination of voice, action, and reflection. Engagement exists when individuals recognize that they have responsibilities not only to themselves and their families, but also to their communities—local, national, and global. It exists when they recognize that the health and well-being of those communities is essential to their own health and well-being. They act in order to fulfill those responsibilities and try to affect those communities for the better. Those actions, in turn, give them an even deeper understanding of their interdependence with communities.

The Role of Higher Education in Civic Engagement

The RYV campaign's initial emphasis was to reach as large a group of students as possible through student leaders, changing the culture of campuses along the way. But as the campaign progressed, RYV participants began to see that the original goal of an engaged, active student body could not be realized without some changes in their institutions.

Even the most indefatigable RYV organizers were disappointed at some point by low turnout at an event or by their inability to reach a segment of the student body. Many encountered the barriers to engaging their peers that we outlined earlier. Some came to believe that the existing institutional system was limiting their ability to engage more students. It was possible to continue holding isolated dialogues and service projects and engage a limited group of students, but a concerted commitment to civic engagement that could shift the campus culture and make civic engagement the norm required some institutional change. In this section, we highlight some factors that led students to this conclusion.

Rising Expectations

RYV students were well-positioned to envision what would be possible if colleges shifted the rules, resources, and commitments to facilitate civic engagement. First, as engaged students, RYV leaders had a good a sense of what works—what involves and excites their peers, and what falls flat. Second, many RYV students had undertaken campus mapping projects early in the campaign that left them with a good sense of the structure and purpose of departments and programs. These mapping projects illuminated both institutions' potential to contribute to civic engagement on campus and the ways in which they inhibit civic involvement. With a student perspective and a decent understanding of their institutions, RYV leaders began to consider how the institutions themselves could change to involve more students in community and public work.

Perhaps most important, when RYV leaders met at statewide meetings and at national conferences, they began to hear what other college administrations were doing to support civic engagement. At conferences and regional meetings, students traded information about the types of financial support their schools made available for community work, the collaborations they were able to establish with service-learning professors, and their administrators' level of public commitment to engagement. Regional and national conferences helped students compare existing civic engagement programs and envision an engaged campus.

Through the national RYV network, students in Oklahoma found out about service-learning and realized that not all civic involvement has to take place outside of class. Inspired by what she heard about service-learning, Summer Stowe-Johnson worked with the embryonic service-learning program at her school and helped it grow. James Williams said of his work with Campus Compact, "Just to see the type of work that's happening across the country has really informed the work that I'm doing on campus at Princeton."

A primary concern among many of the students at the Chicago conference was that their institution's commitment to preparing students for a job or career far outweighed its commitment to preparing students to be active, effective participants in civil society. For example, as RYV students began to explore social issues—poverty, education, racism, and others—outside the classroom, some were disturbed that they had never encountered discussions of these issues *in* the classroom. One student in Chicago put it this way: "At the end of four years, many students are equipped with a degree in one hand and a stable job in the other, but lack the tools necessary to become citizens in our democracy." RYV participants recognized a preparation gap in their education that, if not filled, would leave them and their classmates vulnerable in a complex world that faces a host of global challenges—both in their jobs and in their communities.

As a student, it is intimidating to approach administrators or faculty to suggest changes to the structure of the institution. While many RYV leaders saw what might be possible on their campuses, only a few were able to effect institutional change. At the University of California at San Diego, Emily Yee helped create a student staff position at her community service center to ensure that a student is always involved in planning and leading civic engagement projects. Yee even changed her career path in order to pursue further institutional reforms in higher education.

Yee and others took steps to strengthen their schools' overall support for civic engagement. While it wasn't the central focus of the Raise Your Voice campaign at the start, we now see students' heightened expectations of their educational experience as one of the campaign's biggest successes. As students looked for ways to engage more of their peers, they began to articulate what they believe an undergraduate education should encompass.

Why Civic Engagement?

With so many other priorities, why should colleges and universities encourage civic engagement? During the past 20 years, many scholars have tackled this question. We don't propose to delve into all the intricacies of this issue here. Instead, we expect to contribute to the ongoing conversation by raising relevant issues that come from the RYV experience and from a student point of view.

PREPARATION FOR LIFE

Students need to be prepared for all aspects of public life—not only careers but democratic life as well. In asking for a civic as well as a professional education, RYV students came to the same conclusions as renowned educational advocate Ernest Boyer. Boyer stressed the importance of "an undergraduate experience that helps students go beyond their own private interests, learn about the world around them, develop a sense of civic and social responsibility and discover how they, as individuals, can contribute to the larger society of which they are a part" (1987, pp. 67–68). Across the board, RYV students said they wanted a college experience that prepared them for both a fulfilling job and an active community life.

Some students found that their institutions did just that. Casey Harris commended the University College of Bangor, a campus of the University of Maine at Augusta, for widening his worldview and educating him as a citizen. Harris entered college strictly for career advancement. He had hurt his back and needed a less physically demanding career, so he decided to study computer technology. Once on campus he got involved in RYV and became a civic leader in his community. "At the beginning of Raise Your Voice," he says, "I had nothing to draw on [in terms of] social issues. I lived in my little world and tried to make enough money to support my family. So fair trade…the magnitude of world hunger…all of those things that I have learned about, I had no clue about."

COMMUNITY BUILDING AND DEVELOPMENT
Institutions of higher education are uniquely positioned to create engaged community members and stronger communities. Higher education has the resources, both intellectual and material, to support community building and community development. Colleges are a major locus of knowledge in our society, and deep, effective civic engagement depends on the knowledge and ability to leverage resources.

United with community-based knowledge, academic knowledge can play an important role in campus-community partnerships. At their colleges and universities, literacy volunteers can become better tutors by taking classes on child development; homeless advocates may discover a new tactic by taking classes on policy and researching city politics. Such learning has a dual effect: the impact the tutor and the advocate have on the world increases, while their classroom learning is enhanced through real-world experiences. The most effective civic engagement is informed engagement, and colleges and communities together have the knowledge that can make social, political, and economic work more informed and effective.

LIFELONG DEMOCRATIC DIALOGUE SKILLS
Aside from research and knowledge, colleges can provide an environment of inquiry and dialogue that is critical for social change. As noted earlier, the best civic engagement initiatives include a component of deliberate dialogue and reflection. As a place of inquiry, questioning, exploration, and learning, the campus is well suited to hosting discussions and reflections on social, economic, and political issues. Higher education offers on unrivaled opportunity to hold these discussions and to learn new concepts, discover how the world works, reconcile multiple viewpoints, and deepen our understanding of difficult and complex issues. These dialogues sow the seeds of mutual understanding and strong, connected communities.

For example, RYV student leader Leah Malave of the University of Maine at Augusta identified a critical campus issue through a communitywide discussion. Seeing women students struggle to balance their educational and childcare responsibilities, Malave and other students started a campus conversation about finding ways to assist women. The topic of their conversation, one central in many women's daily lives, became an issue the local government is now working on to find effective options for women on campus.

The benefits of such activity can be broad and lasting. When colleges and universities build the skills of dialogue and reflection, they give on- and off-campus communities the opportunity to discuss and work through critical issues. Graduates then take these skills to their own communities and their daily personal and professional lives.

STRONGER CAMPUS COMMUNITY

Well-run civic engagement programs foster strong communities on campuses and encourage a deep connection to classroom learning. When students find interesting, exciting ways to be civically engaged, the overall campus community becomes stronger. Civic engagement replaces students' detachment with dedication. Many students at the Chicago conference reported that the RYV campaign created a new sense of dedication and community on campus. An RYV leader from Montana spoke eloquently of how the RYV efforts at her tribal college rekindled a sense of community and excitement on her campus, where hopelessness had become entrenched.

This sense of community can both improve the learning atmosphere and build long-term school loyalty. One student said that being engaged "changed the way I think about my university." He had disliked his campus and said, "I thought nobody gave a damn about anything, and it scared me . . . but after RYV . . . I no longer think that."

ENHANCED EDUCATION

When the social and political issues that students care about outside the classroom are tied to academic work, students respond with passionate interest. As noted earlier, RYV students only rarely organized through the curriculum. But many students suggested that a truly engaged education would intertwine academic and civic work. RYV leader Emily Garr of Emerson College said, "You can do all the organizing work you want. You're not going to reach kids . . . unless you create a space where the work you're doing is somehow beneficial to your educational experience."

For reasons discussed earlier, it was difficult for RYV students to initiate service-learning or participatory learning in their schools. Although students wanted to connect their community work with their academic fields, most could not do so and therefore could not comment on the effectiveness of this strategy. But researchers have shown that courses incorporating all three aspects of civic engagement—action, reflection, and voice—not only result in more effective community work but improve students' academic learning as well (Eyler, Giles, Stenson, & Gray, 2001).

RYV students praised those who educate students not simply to be professionals but to be "civic professionals." Kelli Wolf lauded her administration at Missouri State University for introducing incoming students at convocation to the idea that "when you graduate from MSU, you need to be a 'citizen biologist' or a 'citizen teacher.'" In other words, in any profession, graduates should be able to reflect on the impact of their actions and make ethical choices that promote the public good.

Envisioning the Engaged Campus

Imagine a college campus that is deeply committed to civic engagement. On this campus, respectful dialogue about public issues resonates through residence halls, public spaces, and classrooms. Disagreements are common, but people struggle to listen to and understand other points of view. A sense of commitment and purpose is palpable among students and among administrators, staff, and faculty. Students find enjoyable, fulfilling ways to contribute to the public good, which intersect with their course of study. There is constant activity around campus as students and others work on service projects, activist campaigns, policy advocacy, and community-based research.

In administrative offices and program centers, staff members and administrators solicit and value students' opinions. Because of these forums, students feel that they own their education, and especially their civic learning. Rather than a responsibility thrust on them, they see civic engagement as something they can choose and shape to fit their own lives and interests.

Graduates of this school leave the campus community as active and engaged citizens. As businesspeople, public servants, nurses, or chemists, these graduates bring a strong commitment to society into their fields. Outside the workplace, they raise the quality of public dialogue in our country, use their knowledge of public issues to hold legislators accountable, and contribute to community improvement. They go on to build a society in which more people live in a respectful, responsible, and civil way.

This school does not yet exist, but some colleges and universities are beginning to resemble it. From RYV students' many suggestions, commendations, and criticisms, we have crafted a picture of how these potential benefits can be realized. If higher education institutions are to develop a civically engaged culture based on the democratic values of pluralism, equality, and social justice, they must both model civic engagement and work to engage people in the campus community.

As examples from the most engaged schools show, creating a culture of engagement requires significant institutional commitment. In reviewing these examples, we have identified seven steps that can help create that commitment and lead to a vibrant atmosphere of civic engagement and socially responsible action on campus. Some of these steps may depend on the decision of a single person; others are long-term processes. However, each should be one piece of a larger vision tailored to your own campus and community.

1. Create a Central Resource for Engagement

While different departments and programs can house their own civic engagement work, it is extremely useful to have a central place where students can find out about all civic engagement opportunities and communicate and discuss strategy. When engagement opportunities are available in a single location, students can get involved easily and use resources efficiently.

At the University of Utah, for example, community service, service-learning courses, and other engagement opportunities are all coordinated through the Lowell Bennion Community Service Center. Recently, the center has branched out from coordinating service and service-learning to housing community-based research projects and political activism as well. This centralized approach to civic engagement allows students to choose freely among many projects and types of engagement to find a good match, avoiding fragmentation and isolation among projects.

Many colleges and universities are moving in this direction. According to Campus Compact's annual member survey, 86% of the organization's nearly 1,000 member campuses had an office or center dedicated to coordinating service, service-learning, and/or civic engagement activities and programs (Campus Compact, 2006). Others have created online databases of volunteer and other engagement opportunities. Full coordination among all types of engagement activity is not yet the norm, however.

2. Increase Course-based Civic Learning and Service-Learning

A critical step to creating a civically engaged campus is to support engagement in the classroom. The concept of service-learning has existed for decades, supported by extensive research and analysis to determine the benefits and best practices. As students, we too believe that students stand to benefit from this type of education. This pedagogy allows students to apply civic and professional knowledge in a real-world setting, giving them valuable practical experience, while they benefit and learn from the community. In addition, when service and academic learning are blended with critical reflection, civic and service-learning are powerful tools to spark students' interest and involvement in public issues.

Portland State University, for example, provides faculty with mini-grants to develop new service-learning courses. Additional mini-grants are awarded for integrating more comprehensive reflection and assessment into service-learning courses. Faculty members receive extensive support to develop scholarship related to their service-learning, including promotion and tenure policies that reward community service scholarship.

Where service-learning is in place across a department, it can have a much greater impact than one or two service-learning courses isolated from the rest of the academic experience. At Chandler-Gilbert Community College in Arizona, service-learning is an integral part of the curriculum in the general education classes. Throughout their education, students participate in a variety of service events at various community and nonprofit agencies in order to receive a real-world education.

3. Honor and Create Opportunities for Student Input

If we have learned anything from the RYV campaign, it is that a culture of passionate engagement flourishes when students have a voice in their civic engagement work and in their campus community. Incorporating student voice is a challenge that higher education should welcome. When students have input into their own work, they learn leadership skills, feel ownership of their civic engagement projects, and contribute a valuable perspective.

Student input can take many forms. Schools can allow students to vote on campus committees, participate in meaningful administrative discussions, take leadership roles in fostering community partnerships, and design service-learning classes. RYV students at the Chicago conference talked about the new ground they had broken by getting their institutions to hire a student staff person in a community service office, to include students on committees, and to hold student-administrator dialogues. Other students have taken on leadership roles in the classroom (see *Students as Colleagues: Expanding the Circle of Service-Learning Leadership*, Zlotkowski, Longo, & Williams, 2006). These students were enthusiastic about their institutions' progress and eager to work on behalf of their own constituents—the student body.

4. Build Stronger Community Partnerships

Education institutions serve as role models for how to practice democracy. Higher education should refrain from making "token gestures," which "have a damaging effect on the greater student population," notes Stephen Chan, an RYV student leader from Stanford University. Instead, they should work to create strong community partnerships built on reciprocal and sustainable relationships.

The Campus Compact publication *Benchmarks for Campus/Community Partnerships* (2000) presents three stages characteristic of genuine democratic partnerships. In stage one, campus and community organizations work toward "designing partnerships based on the values of sharing and reciprocity." Stage two involves "building collaborative work relationships among partners." Stage three focuses on sustainability—"linking partnerships to the missions of the partnering institutions, establishing processes for decision making and problem solving, and installing the mechanisms for continuous evaluation" (p. 5). Through strong community partnerships, institutions can exemplify democratic practice while teaching students through this step-wise process.

5. Make Campus Administration Structures Transparent

The inner workings of an institution can be difficult for students to navigate. Making the system transparent tells students that they are respected and allows them to navigate power structures to bring about change on their campuses and in their communities.

We recognize that institutions of higher education are unlikely to become less fragmented or simpler. The inevitable yet convenient divisions among departments and other bodies make it even more important that administrators educate students about the workings of the institution. Brief printed or online guides for civically engaged students are immensely useful. If students are organizing a lecture, dialogue, or service trip, or founding a new student organization, where do they go for assistance? What phone numbers will they need? What permission slips and signatures are required? Other strategies to support transparency include annual training or orientation for new leaders and freshmen or detailed job descriptions for staff and administrators.

6. Increase Support for Staff and Faculty Who Do Engaged Work

Faculty and staff who support campus engagement should be rewarded for their efforts. Making faculty and staff eligible for promotion based on their commitment to student and community engagement will strengthen their commitment to the institution and provide a strong incentive for engaged work.

In "Models of Good Practice for Service-Learning Programs," Mary Kay Schneider (1998) quotes a survey respondent from the University of Maryland as saying, "Top administrative support, especially our president, has made resources available to support a successful program, which has led to a highly motivated and talented staff to coordinate our large, comprehensive service-learning program." This type of support from the top can make a huge difference in campus culture and practice.

7. Create Systemic Reforms to Support Civic Engagement

We believe that institutions must create reforms to inspire civically engaged learners who combine academic and civic knowledge in their professional and community lives. Campus Compact's *Presidents' Declaration on the Civic Responsibility of Higher Education* (see www.compact.org/resources/detail.php?id=35), signed by more than 500 college and university presidents, allows us to believe that there is some awareness that institutional change is necessary. We ask only that students be part of the collaborative process that brings about this change.

According to Irwin Altman (1996), Distinguished Professor of Psychology at the University of Utah, who has had a major impact on the university's undergraduate curriculum:

> We must craft new relationships between faculty, between institutions, and the communities that we serve. This does not mean that we reject traditional teaching and research values. It does mean, however, that we carefully assess society's needs now and in the future and that we reshape our educational activities to meet the emerging needs of the decades to come. (p. 374)

We all have a duty to make higher education about more than textbook knowledge. College is a place where we gain the life knowledge that will assist us in developing into the people we want—and need—to become. College is also uniquely positioned to engage students and communities to understand and address the challenges in our democracy. In short, higher education is an ideal forum for exploring new ways of fulfilling the promise of justice and dignity for all, both in our own communities and as part of the global community.

How to Begin

It's not enough merely to envision our ideal college campuses. We need to have a detailed plan to get there. Raise Your Voice taught students that they have the ability to change their institutions, and that they have a stake in creating schools that give them the civic education more and more students are demanding.

If we want to do this in a way that will make other students, staff, faculty, administrators, college communities, and legislators sit up and listen, then it's time for us to agree to organize—to work together on our campuses, within our states, and nationwide. We propose the following ideas about what the student movement for institutional change might look like.

Strategies for Individual Students

1. Make civic engagement a priority. This doesn't mean you instantly need to become a super-student who lobbies, volunteers, leads student organizations, and wears thrift-store clothing. It just means that you should try to go one step farther in the way you contribute to your community, keeping in mind the principles of voice, action, and reflection. If you're already a committed volunteer or a passionate political lobbyist, try a different form of engagement for a while. You never know what you might learn.

2. Ask questions and build relationships. Take some time to get to know your campus and community. What is the name of the custodian you run into every morning in the hallway, and what is she or he passionate about? What kinds of people live in the houses around the campus, and what do they think of the students? How many student organizations exist on campus? Why exactly does the administration ban streaking at the pre-exam midnight breakfast?

To learn how your college works, take five minutes to chat with someone you might not otherwise talk to or poke around your school website to figure out what all those administrative offices do. You might learn about an issue that inspires people on campus or find an office that will help you write a press release. The relationships you form through your conversations will be invaluable as you continue to work toward building an engaged campus.

3. Find a mentor. Sometimes we just need someone to support what we are doing or to believe that we are capable of achieving our goals. A good mentor will do this, while being truthful about our skills and able to give pointers on how to capitalize on our strengths. A good mentor also knows when to let go, and we can all use help with that. There are people who will willingly share their insight and wisdom. Most of these individuals want to affect at least one person in their lifetime.

Staff or faculty members are especially useful mentors. They respect one another on a level that is not always afforded to students, and they can use this leverage to help you accomplish a goal. They know the system they work within, and they can help provide information and resources that may be hard for you to obtain on your own.

4. Connect with similarly committed individuals. Other engaged students can energize and enlighten you. Being around people who continue to challenge you is helpful. You can bounce ideas off of other people and hear new ideas you may not have thought of.

Strategies for Campus Groups

1. Know your stuff. As a campus group, learn about your campus through mapping before choosing your two or three priorities for the year. As an organizer, always make sure you have as much information as you can on your issue before meeting with other students, staff, faculty, administrators, or community members. Being knowledgeable will not only will save you time and effort but also help you to gain the respect of decision makers.

Getting to know your campus will also allow you to identify possible resources and allies. Knowing who does what will help when you're organizing or want to resolve a particular issue.

2. Find or create avenues for passing on knowledge. You don't have to reinvent the wheel every time you look for information or have a great idea about a project. Capitalize on people's institutional memory to get ideas. Your project may have been done before; guidance can save you time and hassle. Find older students who have taken on projects similar to yours, or faculty or staff who have supported student projects in the past. Even if you are doing something different, it can help to talk through your ideas with a seasoned veteran.

If you had to search for information about how to plan community projects and campus events, make sure the students who come after you do not. Find ways to pass on your knowledge. For example, you can create a booklet with relevant information for incoming students; find a permanent faculty or staff person to guide students and to serve as their long-term memory; or institute a regular civic engagement training session through your student government or community service office to teach new students how to navigate the campus structure and implement their ideas.

3. Consider a variety of tactics. When you decide what change you want to make—whether it's bike-rack space for every bike owner on campus or a service-learning requirement in every major at your school—make sure your first approach is to know and work through the expected protocol for meeting and working with administrators. If you succeed, that's great. If you try several times and don't succeed, consider alternative tactics such as lobbying, striking, or going to the media. If you're challenged for doing so, you'll be able to point out that the established system failed you.

4. Collaborate, don't duplicate. Most Raise Your Voice students and groups said that their greatest strength was being able to bring people together to collaborate. Just helping people to organize or connecting your department with the service-learning office can transform civic engagement on your campus. This avoids duplication and capitalizes on limited resources.

When trying to build a coalition that will energize and engage more students, think about how partisanship can help or hinder your efforts. We found that staying nonpartisan or creating a safe space where others can ask questions and learn the things that you may already know was helpful. By being nonpartisan, you can reach everyone, which can be helpful when trying to change the culture of an institution.

State, Regional, and National Strategies

1. Advocate for a state student civic engagement coordinator. Repeatedly, Raise Your Voice students discussed the importance of having the support of a person whose only job was to think about student civic engagement. Campus Compact's state staff can help coordinate statewide activities and support and mentor you in planning local ones. Some state Campus Compact offices employ a student civic engagement coordinator. Check to see if someone is working in this capacity on the RYV website (www.actionforchange.org). If you live in a state that doesn't have a coordinator, you can advocate for one through your institutional board of regents, college president, and student affairs office. The coordinator might be a VISTA volunteer, a graduate employed by several schools, or someone else.

2. Be part of a regional student network. Having a strong state- or regionwide network means that students can train, mentor, and support each other in their work toward civic engagement and institutional change. At the very least, have a good, well-used listserv where you can ask questions about how to recruit volunteers or how different schools' service-learning offices are staffed. Through that network, you can trade successful strategies for getting students involved. You may need to work with your college or university webmaster, but a computer programming student can start the process through an organizational website. If you can, meet face-to-face with other students either regionally or statewide for training or dialogue, using existing conference opportunities or creating your own opportunities. We are our own best resource.

Learning about other schools' civic engagement programs can also help you persuade those at your own campus to make civic engagement a priority. Your campus will be much more willing to create new service-learning classes or put students on administrative committees if you can point to a peer institution that does the same, especially if you can provide information on how it's done and what the benefits are.

3. Collaborate with other campuses. One student at a state house office asking for fair textbook prices can be dismissed as a radical. Fifty students at the state house, representing every higher education institution in the state, are a force to be reckoned with. Raise Your Voice students have their greatest successes in the political arena when students from many different campuses come together to advocate for the same thing.

Intercampus collaboration also attracts publicity for the campaign and gets the message out. State and national media are much more likely to cover a large event or an event occurring on several campuses at once than a small event on only one campus. Positive publicity for a college will make administrators happy, which gives you an advantage in your negotiations with them.

4. Connect with a national network of student leaders. Find people who have a national perspective on student civic engagement and try to attend national student events. National organizations have been created for nearly every issue possible. If you don't know about these organizations, use a keyword search engine.

Participating in a national network will help you on three levels. First, it is inspiring to realize that you are not alone in your commitment to justice and democracy. Second, your campus can learn from similar campuses' successes, and often national organizations can provide detailed information about successful tactics and programs. If you're doing well, you can share your wisdom with others. Finally, through a national network, students can make unified demands and increase their clout in higher education and in society.

Conclusion

These ideas and strategies come from the dedicated students in the Raise Your Voice campaign. This "Lessons Learned" declaration is a resource to get you started on creating change. Not all the information here applies to all situations, and your thinking will no doubt go beyond what we have provided. Use the information to take whatever you are doing to the next level. Use it wisely to effect change in your life, in your community, and on your campus.

References

Altman, I. (1996). Higher education and psychology in the millennium. *American Psychologist,* 51, 371–378.

Boyer, E. (1987). *College: The undergraduate experience in America.* New York: Harper & Row.

Campus Compact (2000). *Benchmarks for campus/community partnerships.* Providence, RI: Campus Compact.

Campus Compact. (2006). *2005 service statistics: Highlights of Campus Compact's annual membership survey.* Providence, RI: Campus Compact.

Center for Information & Research on Civic Learning & Engagement (CIRCLE). (2004). *Youth voter turnout in the states during the 2004 presidential and 2002 midterm elections.* (Available at www.civicyouth.org/PopUps/FactSheets/FS_04_state_vote.pdf.)

Eyler, J.S., Giles, D.E., Stenson, C.M., & Gray, C.J. (2001). *At a glance: What we know about the effects of service-learning on college students, faculty, institutions, and communities, 1993–2000* (third edition). Nashville, TN: Vanderbilt University. (Available at www.compact.org/resources/aag.pdf.)

Long, S. (2002). *The new student politics: The Wingspread statement on student civic engagement.* Providence, RI: Campus Compact.

Schneider, M.K. (1998, June). Models of good practice for service-learning programs. *AAHE Bulletin.* (Available at http://servicelearning.org/resources/links_collection/index.php?popup_id=894.)

Zlotkowski, E., Longo, N.V., & Williams, J.R. (2006). *Students as colleagues: Expanding the circle of service-learning leadership.* Providence, RI: Campus Compact.

Chapter 2
Community Mapping on Campus

Community mapping is both a tool and a way of life for the best community organizers. Like the other tools in this book, it is an essential civic skill for making positive change. Community mapping can also be the foundation that supports all other student action for change.

Colleges and universities have vast amounts of resources for students. The trick is to find those resources and use them effectively. Whether you want to organize a dialogue or speaker series on campus, find a faculty member to give you academic credit for community service, or change a campus policy on an important issue, mapping is the first step.

Often mapping is done informally; you can do it in your head, without even realizing it. How did you find out what classes to take this semester? You might have asked a friend, talked with your adviser, and then had a discussion with someone who had already taken the class. In this process, you engaged in community mapping to find the right class. You also probably did some version of mapping to decide which colleges to apply to and then which to attend.

This chapter will help you formalize the mapping process and invite others into that process with the explicit goal of allowing you effect change on campus. It begins with a short overview of community mapping and the continuum of ways to use it (including time commitments for various versions). It also gives some historical and contemporary examples of the diversity of ways community mapping has been used.

The core of this chapter, the Mapping Toolkit, offers concrete activities for mapping your campus community. The "Who's Around?" activity is designed to help you find resources for your efforts. This tool provides questions for identifying key people, or stakeholders, as well as sample diagrams for plotting these stakeholders and a series of questions to ask them in interviews. "Helping or Hindering?" lets you look at your school as a potentially engaged institution and determine the strengths and gaps for student voice and student civic engagement efforts. The next activity, "Recommendations for Change," helps you probe what your campus might look like if it were ideally positioned to encourage student engagement and then plan concrete steps to make it happen. The chapter concludes with reflection questions and stories from students who have conducted community mapping on their campuses.

What Is Community Mapping?

Mapping is a tool that initiates a community-building process on campus. When you think of the word *mapping*, you probably think of a street map that tells you where something is located and how to get there. Community mapping does the same thing, except the purpose is to evaluate your campus with regard to student voice and student civic engagement. The map will also help you locate assets for getting involved and making democratic change on your campus. It can help you begin to implement desired civic changes.

In the 1890s, the settlement house pioneers did some of the first community mapping. Jane Addams at Hull House in Chicago did a sociological survey of the neighborhood and published *Hull-House Maps and Papers* (1895). The process developed over time. In the 1930s, some students at Benjamin Franklin Community High School in East Harlem, with support from community-minded principal Leonard Covello, surveyed their neighborhood and then created giant maps that were placed in the school. The maps included information about the number and location of community organizations, public playgrounds, and churches. They also identified places such as liquor stores and bars. In his autobiography, *The Heart Is the Teacher* (1958), Covello writes:

> The map showed that in East Harlem there were forty-one churches and missions, twenty-two political clubs, nine labor organizations, five hundred and six candy stores, and two hundred sixty-two barber shops. There were twenty-eight liquor stores, one hundred fifty-six bars, twenty-six junk shops, six hundred eighty-five grocers, three hundred seventy-eight restaurants, two hundred thirty-two tailors, and sixty-three radio repair shops, as well as two hundred ninety-seven doctors, seventy-four dentists, one hundred and two furniture stores, and fourteen loan offices....
>
> It was both significant and depressing, both to the students and to us as teachers, to realize that a community which could support forty-one religious institutions and twenty-two political clubs and one hundred fifty-six bars could boast only a few open playgrounds for its children, three public halls, and no neighborhood newspaper at all. (p. 53)

More recently, John McKnight and John Kretzmann of the Asset Based Community Development Institute at Northwestern University (www.northwestern.edu/ipr/abcd.html) developed a process of using "asset mapping" for community development and revitalization. They attempted to change the way professionals look at communities. Instead of seeing a community as a glass half empty—looking at all the problems such as drugs, crime, and abandoned housing—they see the glass as half full, mapping community assets such as schools, community centers, and green space.

Harry Boyte and the Center for Democracy and Citizenship at the University of Minnesota (www.publicwork.org) help young people map the power of public issues in communities to create a better understanding of the interests of stakeholders. In the center-sponsored youth initiative, Public Achievement (www.publicachievement.org), young people use mapping to analyze stakeholders and power, build relations among allies, and develop strategies for public works projects.

Using Community Mapping

We have created the community mapping toolkit that follows to help you identify potential assets and allies on your campus and determine the gaps. After the initial mapping, you will be able to develop strategies for action and find additional resources to promote student involvement and the issues you care about.

The mapping toolkit is layered so that it can be used either for a quick analysis or as a means of longer-term community mapping of campus-community connections. Some students will stop after the initial mapping and have some recommendations for action based on that assessment; others will see the initial mapping as simply the start of an intensive mapping process on campus. Both will be valuable and useful.

While many organizers use a mapping process for a specific issue or problem they have identified, the material in this chapter is designed for students interested in using mapping to identify issues, build community, and develop a holistic strategy for student empowerment. You may already be part of a strong campus community, have identified an issue, and wish to use mapping as a way to better understand the context of an issue. You can tailor this process to do mapping that is specific to one issue.

We suggest organizing a campus mapping project with a group of 5 to 25 students from a single campus. Finding the right group depends on you and your campus: you may organize it with students in a class or your residence hall, a student organization on campus, members of student government, or even a group of friends.

We also recommend you seek the help of the community service or service-learning director on your campus or a sympathetic faculty member. They have an institutional memory and can inform you of the history and the tradition of student voice and activism on your campus.

After you've completed the initial community mapping, there are many ways to proceed, including conducting interviews, holding conversations with other students who are mapping their campuses, hosting regional conversations about your institutions, writing an article for the student newspaper, meeting with faculty and or administrators, or presenting your map to a group of community partners. Each of these activities will help build support for your work. See the sidebar on p. 52 for some examples of how mapping has been used on campus.

Mapping Toolkit

The community mapping activities that follow (without the interviews) can be completed in less than two hours. If you do the interviews, each will probably take about a half-hour. You should think of mapping as community building; how much time you spend will vary depending on how you approach community building.

Activity 1: Who's Around?

STEP 1: MAPPING STAKEHOLDERS

During mapping, you may want to fill out the survey individually and then work in groups to draw a map of your campus. You may wish to start with general information (such as the Service-Learning Center) and then be more specific and include names and contact information for people on campus (for example, the center's director and his or her phone number). It is better to be more specific, especially as you begin to interview people you have identified.

A stakeholder is any person or group that has a real interest (or stake) in something. So begin by asking the following questions:

- Who are key stakeholders (on campus and beyond) for increasing student voice and civic engagement opportunities? Who has a real interest in engaging students? (Think about student organizations, key community partners, community service staff, faculty, student affairs administrators, and so on. List them, along with roles and responsibilities.)

- Where are student involvement and action supported (include volunteering, service-learning centers, and political and community work)? (List them, along with specifics about kinds of involvement.)

- What student groups are organizing on campus? (List briefly, explaining the roles or missions of these organizations.)

- Where do students have voice on campus (for example, student government, forums on campus, students on advisory committees)? Who are key student leaders? What do they appear to accomplish? (List them and give examples.)
- Which communities and neighborhood organizations can or do students partner with? (State the primary mission or work of these organizations. Also, find out approximately how far the organization is from campus and how it can be accessed, exploring such issues as transportation, political affiliation, and familiarity or unfamiliarity to students.)

Figure 2-1 shows a blank community mapping chart that you can use to begin mapping out various stakeholder groups.

STEP 2: CONDUCTING INTERVIEWS

Interviews are important for building relationships with key people on campus and finding leverage points for change. They are essential to understanding power on campus, creating allies, and determining how to accomplish a specific goal—anything from hosting a dialogue to encouraging more students to join your

FIGURE 2-1: **Community Mapping Chart**

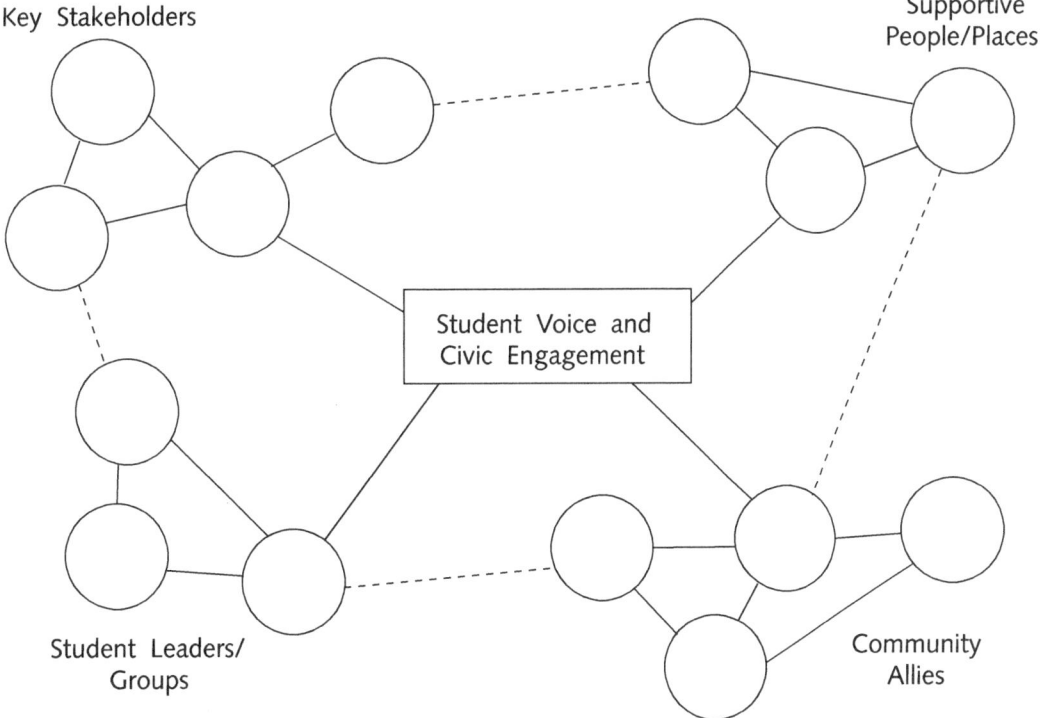

organization to getting your college or university to pay a living wage to its workers.

Be aware that interviews require a lot of time. After the initial mapping, identify the key people on your list and focus on interviewing them. Following are some suggested questions. You should not limit yourself to these questions; let your need for specific knowledge and the work of the person you're interviewing guide what you ask.

- How did you first become involved in your work? (Depending on how the person is identified as a stakeholder, you can ask a more specific question about the organization or civic engagement work in which this person is involved.)
- What drives you to be involved?
- How can we increase student involvement and voice on campus? Do you feel that there is a need to increase student involvement? Why (or why not)?
- What changes would you like to see on campus or in the broader community? Do you think change is possible? How can students play a strategic role in bringing about this change?
- Do you know someone else who is working on these issues?

Follow up on interesting answers and observations. Build on what your interviewee has already said, rather than following a set script. An interviewee who feels listened to is likely to talk more than someone who feels ignored. People like to talk about their work, so this activity, while sometimes daunting, should be fun and meaningful. Try to find out what motivates this person to be involved and how he or she might be enlisted as an ally in your efforts.

Activity 2: Helping or Hindering?

We suggest doing this next activity with other students on your campus. It is a good opportunity to reflect on what has occurred on your campus—even in the recent past—to address factors that support or hinder student civic engagement.

As you look at the people and places you identified (and possibly interviewed) in the first activity, think about the assets and challenges on your campus for fostering student voice and student civic engagement. Specifically, how does your college or university support student voice and student civic engagement? What hinders student participation? What are the challenges? Use the following questions to guide your discussion in determining the assets (or strengths) and the challenges (or gaps) on your campus. The chart in Figure 2-2 can help you map the answers.

- What strengths or assets support student voice and student civic engagement?
- In what areas is your campus strong in its support?
- How does your university show its support?
- What gaps hinder student voice and civic engagement?
- In what areas does your campus need more opportunities for student voice and/or civic engagement?
- How does your university hinder student voice and/or civic engagement?

FIGURE 2-2: **How Does Your College or University Help or Hinder Student Voice and Civic Engagement?**

HELP	HINDER

Activity 3: Recommendations for Change

STEP 1: IMAGINING THE IDEAL CAMPUS

This is a chance to dream about your campus as it should be and come up with a plan to make it happen. Ask yourself the following questions:

- Ideally, how could your college or university help support student civic engagement and foster student voice?
- What concrete steps need to be taken to create a more democratic culture for student voice and civic engagement on your campus? (List as many as you can think of, then prioritize them by importance and achievability.)

Community Mapping Models—Campus Examples

COURSE-BASED MODELS

At **Castleton State College,** students conducted a community mapping project as part of their work in the Community Action Seminar, a newly created sociology class for junior and senior sociology and social work majors interested in civic engagement. In the course, students create and carry out community projects that respond to the needs and social problems of the community.

The class organized and implemented a Raise Your Voice Student Forum during the first half of the semester to help students express their needs. Action groups were formed to follow up on identified problems. For the community mapping project, completed in the second half of the semester, students divided into two groups: the Social Assets Mapping Group and the Power Mapping Group. Each team worked independently in class and outside the classroom. Students presented their results to the president's cabinet at the college.

At **Michigan State University,** students in a class called "American Thought and Language" mapped their community with the support of their professor, who had experience with academic service-learning, and a graduate assistant from the Michigan State University Service-Learning Center. Michigan Campus Compact also provided assistance. Curriculum updates and further information were posted on websites created for the mapping project. Each student's work was documented in online "webfolios" as the project progressed.

STUDENT LEADERSHIP MODEL

Maggie Sventek, a student leader from the University of Minnesota, worked with faculty members and student groups across campus to map civic engagement opportunities on campus. The mapping project was part of her larger work as a Minnesota Campus Compact (MCC) Student Fellow.

Sventek met individually with faculty from a number of departments, including public policy, political science, women's studies, philosophy, and English. She also conducted an email survey of more than 300 student groups probing civic engagement and the connections between the individual groups and the larger Twin Cities communities. She compiled her findings into a mapping project report, which she posted online and presented to a panel of future MCC Student Fellows. To support her efforts, Sventek received four credits through the political science department.

INSTITUTIONAL LEADERSHIP MODEL

The **University of Massachusetts (UMass) Boston** recently charged a subcommittee of the Urban Mission Coordinating Committee (chaired by the Chancellor) with taking an inventory of the outreach, research, and teaching projects connected with communities. The information will be used to create a new Urban Research and Outreach Center, funded in part by a COPC grant from the U.S. Department of Housing and Urban Development.

During the inventory process, the subcommittee designed several survey tools with different focuses, one of which was geography. The group compiled data from several of the projects onto a GIS map unveiled at the first of three events designed to bring UMass faculty, staff, students, and community partners together to discuss the university's strategies for maintaining and promoting partnerships, engaged learning, research, and teaching.

STEP 2: CREATING AN ACTION PLAN

Once you know how you'd like to proceed, you need to follow through on the action steps you have identified. You might share your list of ideas with others on campus, including faculty, staff, administrators, and other students. Think about what is already going on and include people with similar interests and goals.

It's important to build support for your efforts. One strategy is to host campus dialogues on the issue you care most deeply about. You could cosponsor a dialogue with the people you interviewed to generate interest and momentum. (See Chapter 3 for information on hosting dialogues on campus.)

It is also helpful to publicize your assessment of the campus. Options include:

- Write a letter to the student newspaper.
- Meet with faculty and administrators to present your assessment and recommendations.
- Ask your student government to sponsor your mapping and fight for your recommendations.

Discuss your assessment with students from other local campuses and peer institutions to compare notes.

Reflection Questions

During the mapping, it is important to step back and reflect on the process and the results of your assessments. The following questions will help you gauge how the process has affected you personally and your work on campus.

Personal Change

- What did you discover about yourself as you did this mapping? Do you feel that you have become part of a community as a result? Do you feel excited or discouraged about the prospects of making your campus more effective in its approach to engagement?
- Do you find yourself thinking differently about your own role as a student leader or activist?
- How did you share with the stakeholders what you discovered? Were they receptive? What was their reaction?
- What are your hopes and dreams about raising student voice on your campus?

Institutional Change

- In what areas on your campus is student voice and civic engagement strong? (Include as many specific details as possible.)
- What are some obstacles to student voice and student civic engagement on your campus?
- What are your recommendations for creating more opportunities for student voice and civic engagement on your campus?
- What action steps have you taken or will you take to increase student civic engagement?

The answers to these questions will help guide—and enhance—your activity on campus.

References

Addams, J. (1895). *Hull-House maps and papers: A presentation of nationalities and wages in a congested district of Chicago.* New York: T.Y. Crowell.

Covello, L. (1958). *The heart is the teacher.* New York: McGraw-Hill.

Chapter 3
Civic Dialogues

Dialogue is a civic skill that involves much more than just talking or waiting to talk. It involves being able to create free space where others feel comfortable sharing their views. It involves active listening. And it involves organizing.

> *"All social change begins with a conversation."*
> MARGARET J. WHEATLEY (2002)

This chapter will help you democratize your campus by creating public forums, learning circles, and deliberative conversations among your peers, faculty, staff, administrators, and community residents. It contains all you need to know to host, organize, and lead a dialogue on your campus.

Dialogues involve big conceptual issues and abstract conversations; talking through differences on matters of public importance; and creating a safe setting, with the right people in the room, so that change can happen. Thus, dialogues are best organized by teams of students who can complement one another, along with support from staff. Someone needs to work on the details—finding space, publicizing, recording, and following up on the dialogue. At the same time, someone needs to think strategically about how the dialogue connects with other organizing initiatives on campus. In fact, getting the right people to attend your dialogue is almost as important as what happens at the event. It is also helpful to think about bigger issues: How does this conversation relate to the very meaning of democracy, social justice, and civic engagement?

This chapter is organized into several sections, beginning with tools for planning and hosting a dialogue. Logistics "how-to's" include everything from reserving a room to publicizing the event to creating a follow-up action plan. A facilitation discussion includes step-by-step training on skills, tools, and tips for promoting open, interactive, and honest discussions on critical issues.

This chapter also includes an array of sample dialogues that you can use to help focus your topic, plan your activities, or borrow ideas from. The samples offer background information on the proposed topics, as well as an extensive collection of activities and forms, ready for you to use or modify to fit your local environment. (Many of these are also available for download from the Raise your Voice website, www.actionforchange.org/dialogues/forms.html.) To show what this looks like on the ground, we also provide short examples of actual dialogues from campuses around the country. The chapter concludes with a list of organizations and websites where you can find additional resources on hosting dialogues.

The Purpose of Dialogue

"[P]olitics is about relationships that enable people to disagree, interrupt, confront, and negotiate, and through this process of conversation…to forge a consensus or compromise that makes it possible for them to act."
ERNESTO CORTÉS, JR. (1994)

One of the primary tools used by the Raise Your Voice campaign has been civic conversations, or dialogues. Student-led dialogues on a wide variety of topics have been held on college and university campuses across the country. Dialogues among students put them at the center of understanding, allowing them to express their concerns, thoughts, and sentiments, while better understanding the views of other students.

In many cases, dialogues not only helped students *raise* their voice, they also helped people *find* their voice first. Dialogues have aided students in identifying critical issues of mutual concern and places to begin action campaigns. They have been used to demonstrate the inclusiveness of the "Student Action for Change" agenda, as well as to educate a campus on an issue or a set of issues. Student dialogues are the chief means by which Raise Your Voice and many other campaigns have heard the voices of students.

Dialogue differs from debate in that all participants put their own conclusions on hold and regard other participants as colleagues searching for common ground. Facilitators have the task of moving the discussion forward and making sure all voices are heard.

All dialogues have a number of common purposes:
- To bring together people from diverse backgrounds and experience.
- To open avenues for discussion, learning, and cooperation.
- To promote understanding of different viewpoints.
- To identify information or issues.
- To offer opportunities for people to become part of an interactive network of active and concerned citizens.

- To explore, discuss, and carry away for further thought a range of viable alternatives.

Dialogues are *not*:
- Argumentative debates.
- Meetings of, or lectures by, experts.

The Raise Your Voice campaign used dialogues as a way to create safe spaces for student voice on campus, to tap into the passion, power, and wisdom that each person brings, and to connect and catalyze students on campus. We hope you use them in this spirit.

Planning a Dialogue

Sharing the thinking and the work increases the likelihood of a successful dialogue. Two or more students should work together to plan and host dialogues, along with one or more campus advisers who can give you helpful information about how to get things done within the institution. Knowledge about how to navigate campus bureaucracies takes time to develop, and an experienced faculty or staff member can save you valuable time and help you avoid errors.

As a planner, you will have to make many strategic decisions about the type, size, format, and facilitation of your dialogue. While the sample dialogues provided later offer a good range of approaches, there are many other ways of organizing and leading discussions that contribute to public understanding of critical issues. As an organizer, you will want to think about some of the opportunities and challenges that lie before you:

- What shape will the dialogue take? What topic will serve as its focus? What is its objective? What format will be most useful? How many people will it include?
- What occasions serve as ideal moments around which to focus dialogues?
- Who should we invite or include as participants?
- Where should we hold the dialogue?
- What sort of record should we maintain?
- How should we publicize the dialogue?

See the following Dialogue Planning Checklist and Dialogue Planning Form for help as you work through these issues.

Dialogue Planning Checklist

(Use with or instead of the Dialogue Planning Form.)

PRE-DIALOGUE RESEARCH

- Discuss your dialogue ideas with two to four other students for input; consult with campus leaders to weigh the pressing issues and hot topics on campus.
- Check with one or two faculty or staff members to get their input.
- Watch the news to see if there are stories that you can draw on to situate your debate in contemporary and, in particular, local issues.
- Decide on the topic, objectives, and format for discussion. Will there be introductory activities or introductions of participants? Small group work? Activities?
- Be sure that you are comfortable with the topic. Another student, faculty, or staff member can lend expertise if necessary during the dialogue.
- Plan the agenda.

PRE-DIALOGUE LOGISTICS

- Determine the best size for the group and the best participants to target.
- Set a day, time, and length for the session.
- Ask your Student Affairs Department if there are rules governing such meetings.
- Reserve a room or location that you think will enhance the dialogue.
- Invite students to participate. Remind them on the eve of the event.
- Invite one or more faculty or staff members to join you as guests. Remind them on the eve of the event.
- Publicize the event widely.
- Designate someone in advance to serve as recorder.
- Create a sign-in sheet with space for email addresses.
- Designate a facilitator.
- Decide how you (or someone else) will introduce the dialogue and set the guidelines forconversation to ensure democratic practice.
- Prepare any materials you may need for the session (handouts, easel, markers, etc.).
- Decide whether you will offer food or beverages (check rules on facilities to see if these are allowed).
- Determine who will clean up.

(An electronic copy of this checklist is available at ww.actionforchange.org/dialogues/forms.html.)

Dialogue Planning Form

(Use with or instead of the Dialogue Planning Checklist.)

TOPIC

Goal or Objective:　　　　　　　　　　　　Date:

Facilitator(s):　　　　　　　　　　　　　　Time:

Recorder:　　　　　　　　　　　　　　　　Duration:

Day:　　　　　　　　　　　　　　　　　　Location:

FORMAT

Open Issue ___　　Guided Issue ___　　Town Hall ___　　Public Policy ___　　Other ___

PARTICIPANTS

Approximate Number: _____

Characteristics:

Other invited guests or experts:

Press and public relations:

Audiovisual material:

Refreshments:

AGENDA AND FACILITATION ROLES

Introduction and Ground Rules:　　　　　　Evaluation:

Framing the Topic:　　　　　　　　　　　　Clean-up:

Introductory Activity:　　　　　　　　　　Follow-up:

Discussion:　　　　　　　　　　　　　　　Reporting out:

Wrap-up:　　　　　　　　　　　　　　　　Next steps:

(An electronic copy of this form is available at www.actionforchange.org/dialogues/forms.html.)

The Structure

Dialogue structure can vary widely depending on what topic is discussed and for what purpose, who attends and how many, and what format you use. Each of these factors should be considered carefully to make sure the dialogue takes the shape you want it to.

SELECTING A TOPIC

Choosing a topic for your dialogue will pave the way for many of the other decisions you must make. The overall purpose of Raise Your Voice was to create dialogues in order to hear what students have to say about issues of critical importance to society, so a wide range of topics could be considered. In your planning, look for a topic that encourages open discussion about an issue you think is important.

The topics of the sample dialogues that appear later in this chapter may provide some ideas; however, the best topics will be those of immediate interest to the students on your campus, whether those interests center on some issue in national or international news or a recent hikes in campus parking fees. The key is to choose a topic that will engage participants and serve to educate everyone by allowing them to hear different points of view.

SETTING GOALS

Dialogues can be thought of as one-time events or sustained community-building activities. In some cases, a single dialogue may allow everyone to participate and more or less exhaust the topic being discussed. Other dialogues may be designed as a series, continuing to clarify the issue and deepen participants' understanding of an issue over time. Dialogues may be highly structured, with much advanced planning, guest speakers with a specific expertise, and formal rules, or they may be informal—as simple as a concerned group of students gathered in a dorm room or dining hall having meaningful and respectful conversations about issues that matter to them.

Civic dialogues are typically either process-oriented or goal-oriented. *Process-oriented* dialogues are designed to bring diverse people together and promote understanding of different points of view with no particular efforts to reach consensus or identify courses of action. Issue dialogues, art or film discussions, learning circles, and book clubs are examples. *Goal-oriented* dialogues are designed to establish goals, strategies, and plans for collective action. Town hall meetings and public policy dialogues are often structured in this manner. If it is your goal is to emerge from the dialogue with specific plans, select and structure a topic so that action outcomes are likely to occur.

CHOOSING A FORMAT

One key to planning your dialogue is to determine what format it will take. The following examples offer a range of choices.

Open-issue dialogues are structured around a central theme or question. Only the participants present information. Open-issue dialogues have minimal structure, relying on a single facilitator and a set of basic questions that hinge on one or more issues and invite everyone to participate fully.

Guided-issue dialogues are structured around a body of outside information that sets the stage for the conversation. Information sources may include:

- A speaker (for example, an invited elected official might talk briefly about his or her own work on youth agendas).
- A film or video (for example, a dialogue might follow the screening of a film or video with a civic, service, or political message).
- A book or article (where participants gather to discuss a text chosen in advance and its relationship to their lives).
- An art exhibit (particularly one with civic or political meaning—for example, the work of José Clemente Orozco, which might foster a dialogue about the experience of immigrants in America).
- A panel (for example, a student might join a college administrator, a local nonprofit leader, and a political science instructor in a panel presentation that leads into a dialogue on education, service, and political change).

The *world café* format invites participants to hold small, informal conversations at different tables, each of which has a specific question or topic for conversation. The table is covered with butcher paper and has colored marking pens so people can make notes, draw diagrams, or write their thoughts. After 20–30 minutes, participants move to a different table. One person remains at the table to introduce the topic and convey some of the primary thoughts of the previous group. This process repeats two to four times and concludes with a wrap-up with all the participants.

The key to organizing a good world café dialogue is to design questions that relate to each other without being redundant, so that each round of conversations deepens and expands both the dialogue and the depth of understanding. Organizers should include participants who have facilitation skills to ensure the principles of open dialoguing are honored, even though there is no designated facilitator at each table. A good facilitator who can help participants identify and share insights should conduct the wrap-up.

Open-space (or open-space technology) forums are generally part of a larger meeting, often held over several days. Meeting participants identify topics that they wish to know more about or to further discuss but that do not appear on the formal agenda and set a time for a dialogue. Often someone in the group with expertise on the topic volunteers to initiate the dialogue. Open space is an extemporaneous dialogue that evolves from the interests of participants, allowing them to augment the agenda of their existing event.

A *town hall meeting* is a goal-oriented dialogue that is intended to produce some action or recommendation. For example, students may want to discuss a specific issue such as "student roles in the evaluation of faculty" and emerge from the dialogue with concrete factual understanding of the issue and possibly some recommendations. These meetings generally begin with one or more people clearly articulating the issue.

A *public policy* dialogue, unlike other dialogues, is designed to bring together a representative sampling of different leaders who will move an issue to new levels and shape policy. These gatherings have more of an "expert" flavor than other types of dialogues. For example, leaders from student government, student press, and student organizations might gather for a policy dialogue on "increasing student participation in campus governance."

Learning circles come from a rich tradition of citizen activism and democratic education, including the work of well-known educators such as Paulo Freire and Myles Horton. Learning circles are small, face-to-face gatherings where people build trust and share their ideals, goals, practices, and experiences. Learning circles seek to create free, safe spaces for participants to share their stories and collaboratively discuss topics of personal interest. (For more information about learning circles, see the Educators for Community Engagement website, www.e4ce.org.)

DETERMINING SIZE

What size is ideal for a successful dialogue? Much depends on the format, what organizers hope to accomplish, and the level of agreement or disagreement on the topic. As a general rule, smaller is better, and diversity of opinion is an asset. A good size for an introductory dialogue is 10–15 participants, which allows each participant to join in conversation and lends itself to building relationships and respectful listening.

More formal formats that have narrow topics, possibly introduced by a panel or expert, might be much larger. Town hall meetings might accommodate 100 or more participants.

MAKING USE OF OCCASIONS
Sometimes it seems as if we are a society that lurches from one "special occasion" to the next; it may be useful to take advantage of this tendency by using special events, commemorations, or holidays as a way to structure dialogues. This strategy ties thoughtful deliberation to other experiences and may make deliberation a part of our routines. The anniversary of September 11, 2001, for example, presents an opportunity for dialogue on a range of topics (see Sample Dialogue 3–5 later in this chapter for an example).

Other occasions that lend themselves to dialogue include:

- **Election Tuesday**—Voting: a necessary but insufficient act of citizenship (it might be most valuable to have a dialogue on this topic a week before the close of voter registration).
- **Veterans Day**—Why be patriotic? An exploratory dialogue about patriotism in the "new" America (see Sample Dialogue 3-4).
- **Thanksgiving**—Hunger and homelessness (see Sample Dialogue 3-3).
- **End of year or semester**—Reflections on charity versus change: What can students expect to accomplish through civic action?
- **Martin Luther King, Jr., Day or Cesar Chavez Day**—What can individuals, particularly students, do to work toward social justice? (see Sample Dialogue 3-6).
- **President's Day**—Students and the public good: a dialogue on student involvement in public life (see Sample Dialogue 3-1).
- **Earth Day**—Students' role in creating a sustainable planet.

These are only a few examples of events and possible dialogue topics. Use your own imagination, local or campus events, and the energy of your campus to identify occasions that might be made more notable by including a dialogue.

The Participants

INVITING PARTICIPATION
Although dialogues are intended to bring together a diverse group of participants, a guiding rule is that the people invited should have an interest in the topic and agree to the basic rules of civil discussion. Whom should you invite to participate?

Engaged students—You may wish to begin dialogues with students who are already engaged, such as those involved in community service or campus political activities. They have already thought about civic engagement and have an interest in the dialogue process. Think about including students from diverse backgrounds, including gender, race and ethnicity, sexual preference, and age or year in school.

Selected students—In rare cases, you may want to offer dialogues to a selected group of students if your intention is to use the dialogue to promote some specific policy or goal (see the discussion of public policy dialogues in the previous section).

The unengaged—The most successful dialogues should strive to involve those students who show no obvious interest in public issues. These students can contribute greatly to our understanding of civic participation, as too frequently they are lumped into an apathetic category without efforts to understand why they choose not to participate. These dialogues may be most successful if planned as part of a course, because it is difficult to draw these students to civic forums.

The larger community—Too often, students have conversations among themselves, without including faculty, staff, and members of the larger community. Although the tendency is to lean toward more homogeneous groups of participants (e.g., all students, all students committed to community service, all students who are leaders of community outreach efforts), in general the more diverse the group, the richer the dialogue. But diversity requires a savvy and experienced facilitator to manage potential conflicts. Real problems can occur if the facilitator is a student and the person dominating the floor is a faculty or staff member.

Experts—As you plan, weigh whether it would help to have a subject matter expert join the dialogue. Think about how an expert from on or off campus might help frame an issue and provide clarification. If your dialogue is on a topic such as campus marketing of sweatshop products, you might bring in a student from another school who has been involved in the issue or a reporter who has written stories for the local paper. Think carefully about the role of any expert you invite and be sure that she or he agrees to the limits of their participation. Experts should be "on tap," not "on top"—that is, they should be a resource for the dialogue but not in charge of the conversation. Be sure to consider whether an expert might hamper conversation (e.g., if students are uncomfortable sharing their ideas with campus employees).

GETTING PEOPLE THERE

One way to start the process is to map the stakeholders on your campus and ask them to co-host or attend the dialogue. Stakeholders may differ depending on your dialogue topic and your campus. Ask yourself a few questions to get a quick idea of whom you should invite: What is your issue? Who are the people who have a stake or interest in this issue? Have you considered all stakeholders, both on and off campus?

Think about where stakeholders are located, how you can contact them, and what interest they may have in partnering with you or helping to recruit students to come to your dialogue. People are willing to help; often it requires someone to ask the right question. (You can use the Community Mapping tool in Chapter 2 of this book to identify stakeholders; see Table 3-1, below, for a list to help you get started.)

Once you know who you want to invite, one of the most effective methods of getting people to come is to issue personal invitations. Invite people over the phone and in person as well as posting flyers and sending emails. People who are personally invited are much more likely to attend and to get others to attend. In addition, make reminder phone calls the night before the dialogue to make sure people know that their presence and participation are valued.

TABLE 3-1: **Potential Stakeholders and Where to Find Them**

STUDENTS
- Residence life
- Classes, especially classes with a service-learning component
- Community Service Centers on campus
- Student clubs
- Sororities and fraternities
- Student newspaper

FACULTY
- Academic departments
- Researchers
- Club advisers

STAFF
- Custodial
- Food services
- Secretarial
- Unions
- Security staff

ADMINISTRATORS
- Admissions
- Communications/public relations
- President
- Development
- Dean of students/academics
- Residential life
- Counseling
- Academic development/support

ALUMNI
- Alumni representatives on campus (alumni office)
- Visiting alumni
- Local alumni

BOARD OF TRUSTEES
- Board representatives on campus
- Local or regional board members

LOCAL COMMUNITY
- Local nonprofits
- Government officials
- Community-based organizations
- Local businesses
- Local newspaper
- Local schools—high school students and teachers

Sample Pre-Dialogue Press Release

FOR IMMEDIATE RELEASE

Contact: [Include contact information here]

May 22, 2006

Local College Students Join National Service/Democracy Initiative

St. Lawrence University, Canton, NY — On Friday, May 26, students from St. Lawrence University will meet for a dialogue on student involvement in public life at the Service-Learning Center on campus. This is one of many similar dialogues that are being hosted on campuses across the country as part of a civic engagement initiative sponsored by Campus Compact and funded by The Pew Charitable Trusts. The dialogue will focus on the issue of student action, voice, and power on college campus and in the community.

Although recent studies of voting trends and other indicators continue to label students as passive, disengaged, and uninterested, contradicting studies have repeatedly shown that this generation is more active in public and community service than any past generation. Students see their service within the larger context of addressing social and economic problems through service and political action.

This dialogue will seek to address how student action is an essential role in building a strong democracy, and begin to look at ways student can combine their alternative politics with traditional participation.

This is the first in a series of dialogues designed to get students talking about their work in communities and to explore additional civic strategies. The outcomes will be shared both locally and nationally. More information about this dialoguing initiative can be found at www.compact.org.

SPREADING THE WORD

Dialogue planners must make a strategic decision about whether to publicize a dialogue in advance. For some dialogues, it may be appropriate to extend an open invitation to members of the campus community, including the campus press. Other dialogues should have a limited invitation list so that the number of participants and their backgrounds can be engineered in a way to ensure the dialogue's success. Participants will often talk more freely if the group is small, receptive to the process, and free of observers.

If you are new to hosting dialogues, it is probably better to have a smaller, more controlled event. If you are hosting a town hall meeting, openly inviting students with flier, a story in the campus newspaper, or other public announcement will be more appropriate. The list below offers more ideas about how to get the word out before the dialogue. (For publicity after the dialogue, see the information in the "Press and Public Relations" section later in this chapter.)

Newspapers (campus and local)—You may want to have a story or ad in the newspaper for the event. A press release is an easy, quick way to inform others about your dialogue (see the sample in the sidebar on the opposite page, adapted from an actual press release). When writing a press release, use brief, specific information: Who, what, where, and why, along with your contact information. Then distribute it to any media sources of interest and to professors who may want to mention it in class.

Posters—Campuses are inundated with posters, so be creative. Handmade color posters with marker or crayon may be more eye-catching than fancy black-and-white graphics. If you have the resources, make a big poster. Enlist the help of a graphic artist on campus, check with the art department for screen printers, or make friends with the local copy center's employees.

Radio—Campus radio varies in its usefulness, but it can be an important resource. Have a mini-interview or dialogue on the air, or just ask the station to publicize the event. Most campus radio stations air calendars of events. Other local also stations have calendars of events and are required to read a certain number of public service announcements every day. Airtime on a popular radio station can add a lot of credibility both on and off campus. National Public Radio (NPR) gives airtime and announces events.

Email—Mass campus email (or even paper mail) can be far-reaching but is often ignored. Email is more useful as a way to remind a small group of invited people about the details (where and when the event will be). Email groups and listservs also allow continuation of the dialogue electronically after the event, to include more people as the word spreads. An email list of interested people will make setting up the next dialogue easier.

Web—Setting up a web page, listserv, or message board for the dialogue can give interested people a place to go to exchange ideas.

Personal—One-on-one interaction almost always yields good results. Building relationships can be more useful than building web pages.

The Setting

The success of a dialogue depends partly on where it is held. Consider the following in making your choice:

Comfort—Is the location familiar to participants? Does it lend itself to an atmosphere of respect, equality, and informality? A dialogue around a single large table or a circle or U-shaped configuration is more likely to be successful than one held in a classroom with a facilitator behind a podium.

Access—Whom do you need to ask to reserve the space? What is the process?

Accessibility—Is the location relatively accessible, given the time of day and the transportation available?

Size—Is the size of the facility appropriate for the size of the group? A conference room that accommodates 50 people will seem empty for a group of 16 participants. A room that accommodates 30 will be too cramped for 50 people to engage in comfortable conversation.

Flexibility—Does the space conform to your needs? Can furniture be moved, refreshments brought in, and audiovisual equipment used?

Costs—Can you use the space for free? What is the process for doing so? If there is a charge, how will it be covered?

Audiovisual needs—Whether you are using something as simple as flip-chart or as complex as a movie, you need to anticipate your needs, prepare all the material in advance, and think about where and how to use the material.

Refreshments—Does the facility allow refreshments? Think in advance about where refreshments can be set up; plan on someone to clean up (probably you).

The Record

There are three schools of thought about recording dialogues:

- No written or audio recording of a dialogue should be kept because it inhibits the free participation of attendees.

- A recorder might try to capture the basic ideas and contributions on flipchart paper or a dry-erase board to help people stay focused on the conversation.
- Fairly extensive notes should be taken and an audio recording made to learn the most from the conversation.

As facilitator, the choice is yours. Preserving privacy and promoting the free exchange of ideas is a worthwhile goal, especially if you believe that dialogues are more about the process of engaging students in civic conversations than about what they actually say.

A number of dialogues, however, have demonstrated that the conversations can lead to profound new ways of understanding how fellow students see and understand campus, communities, and public life. Since this requires thorough analyses of the conversations, careful attention to the content of dialogues, captured in written and audio records, is extremely helpful.

Think about how you want to record the dialogue, if at all, and be prepared with whatever material or equipment you need to capture what you have decided is important to document. For a written record of the dialogue, look for a student volunteer (maybe a student from a writing or journalism course). Audio or video equipment can often be rented or used free through the university with faculty or staff permission, but it may be easier to borrow a small recorder from a student, as high-quality recording may not be necessary.

Another method is to meet with the planning team soon after the dialogue to compare notes. This approach is less obtrusive, although not as effective as note taking in capturing the essence of the conversation.

Facilitating a Dialogue

The single most important factor in a dialogue's success is the ability of the facilitator(s) to plan, implement, and evaluate the dialogue. Facilitators must have a clear idea of what they want to accomplish and how they hope to engage other students. Some individuals have a natural ability to be good facilitators. You may find it easier to co-facilitate your dialogue, dividing responsibilities among two, three, or even four student leaders to share in the planning, presentation, and wrap-up (we recommend this approach).

Introducing the Dialogue

SET THE STAGE

Before the dialogue starts, it is helpful for facilitators to mingle, welcoming people and introducing them to one another. If you know some of the participants and can introduce them to others with shared interests or concerns, they can begin to connect right away. The most successful dialogues are those in which people can chat before the beginning of the session.

Try to begin the dialogue close to the appointed time out of respect for those who have shown up on time. Promptness indicates that you take the process seriously and want to make the most of the time available. You may want to start by giving some background about the dialogue's purpose and your connections to any larger campaigns so that participants understand that they are part of a broader conversation.

ESTABLISH THE GROUND RULES

Remember that the fundamental purpose of the dialogue is to search for common ground. Some participants with widely different points of view are accustomed to defending their own position and trying to convince others of the rightness of their beliefs (or to shout down those who do not agree with them). It is critical to set the stage for civil discussion up front. Let participants know that this is not the Jerry Springer show and not a debate in which there will be winners and losers. Lay out the ground rules for conversation in a firm but friendly manner. The basic rules are:

- One person speaks at a time.
- Listen carefully to what others say.
- Give others an opportunity to speak.
- Do not attack or be disrespectful of others.
- Look for what you share in common with others and build on this common ground.

If you have time, rather than dictating the ground rules, you may want participants to suggest their own. They are more likely to adhere to a set of guiding rules they have created themselves.

FRAME THE TOPIC

It is helpful to provide a clear, brief introduction to the topic for the dialogue before the conversation begins. Offer a context for the issue you will be discussing and suggest at least two different sides of the issue. Remind participants that the purpose of the session is to explore many different points of view, to seek common ground, and to better understand other people's opinions.

If the dialogue is more goal-oriented, tell participants what you hope will emerge from the discussion. Be clear about your objective and about the most critical issue—that participants feel free to speak openly about their viewpoints.

Launching the Conversation

After your introduction, allow participants to meet one another in a formal way. If your group is larger than 15 people, you may want to break up the group so you don't use the entire time for introductions.

It is generally not effective simply to go around the room and have people give their name, year in school, and major. One possibility is to ask participants to discuss their service work and attitudes toward public life (see Sample Dialogue 3-1 later in this chapter for an example). Another is to have them define what *civic engagement* means to them and discuss what activities they think constitute engaged work. Such activities give participants a chance to introduce themselves while moving the dialogue forward. (See the following sidebar, From Narrative to Analysis, for another possible activity.)

A word about introductory activities, or "icebreakers": While breaking the ice is critical to any group's success, some icebreakers appear to be based on the idea that participants must be entertained if they are to be engaged. Icebreakers may also delay the work of the meeting instead of moving it forward. Icebreakers can be fun and engaging, but they should be designed to ensure that they contribute to the overall theme and purpose of the dialogue, respect the dignity of student voice, and don't eat up too much time.

Immediately after the introductions is a *prompt* for the dialogue to begin. The prompt focuses the conversation; it may be something simple such as a careful restatement of the dialogue topic, or it may be more complicated, such as a panel presentation, a video, or a dramatic presentation. Whatever you use to provoke the thinking of participants, conclude this section by clearly stating the issue or question for discussion as neutrally as possible and then inviting people to share their points of view.

Guiding the Dialogue

Guiding the dialogue is the facilitator's main job. As a facilitator, you have three basic responsibilities:

- Guiding the dialogue by inviting open and free conversation.
- Keeping the conversation on track.
- Protecting participants from those who abuse the basic ground rules.

As a guide, you must attend to the intellectual quality and emotional atmosphere of the conversation. At the same time, you must know that you cannot expect perfection from yourself or others. Enjoy yourself and invite others to enjoy the process of coming together to talk about issues of civic importance.

Introductory Activity: From Narrative to Analysis

Present a case study of a difficult situation arising from student efforts to organize an event or to make change, or a community service experience that was problematic. Ask the group to analyze the incident.

Example: A university student stood in front of the campus bookstore passing out fliers urging customers not to buy clothing because much of the clothing was from companies using sweatshop labor. A security guard asked the student to move along, as this area of campus was not a "free speech zone." The student claimed that he was not speaking, only passing out fliers and not disturbing anyone. The guard persisted. The student noted that just yards away, a credit card vendor was making much more noise hawking his cards. The guard explained that the vendor had university permission to be there. The student said that as a student at the university, he had a right to be where he was. The guard insisted that political activity was limited to the free speech area. When the student refused to give ground, he was placed under arrest for disturbing the peace, handcuffed, and taken off campus.

(Note: this activity will be more effective if you use an incident from your own campus and/or community rather than the example above.)

Following are some questions you might ask to guide the analysis. Do not feel you need to use all or any of them; feel free to adjust them to better fit your campus, your group, or the situation you are addressing.

1. What were the expectations of the involved parties?
2. What role did communication play in resolving or complicating the situation?
3. Who held the reins of power and what means were used to attempt to counter power?
4. What role did resources or the lack of resources play in the incident?
5. What role might stereotypes have played in the incident?
6. What strategies might have been used by either party to lead to a more positive outcome?
7. How does this incident relate to larger philosophical issues of campus activism or community service?
8. What strategies might be used to ensure that this situation is not repeated?
9. What is the importance of this situation to our understanding of civic engagement?

PROMOTING UNDERSTANDING

Following are ten suggestions for facilitators to keep the conversation moving in a way that promotes understanding among the participants:

1. **Keep the purpose and the goals of the dialogue firmly in mind,** encouraging comments that represent many different points of view yet do not stray too far from the central theme or topic.

2. **Listen carefully** to all comments, trying always to find the common elements or threads that bring people together even when their points seem to be polar opposites.

3. **Ask open-ended questions** that encourage people to elaborate on and clarify their positions. Questions like "What inspired you to become active in the community?" are better than, "Did the Volunteer Center get you interested in community work?"

4. **Remain open-minded and nonjudgmental,** even when participants make comments that you radically disagree with. Perhaps the greatest challenge for the facilitator is to be neutral. It is critical to model good listening and questioning techniques that move the dialogue forward rather than appear to take sides on an issue.

5. **Periodically synthesize or reflect** back major points so that participants can see how comments tie into one another. Make sure that participants feel free to correct you if they do not agree with the way you have restated their points.

6. **Encourage participation** from everyone, attempting to get diverse opinions while making the discussion informative and fun. Make a special effort to get quiet people to speak up. Often they have been listening carefully and have comments that will unite points previously made.

7. **Pace the session,** suggesting when it is time to move on to a new topic, take a break, or have a few minutes of silence so people can integrate ideas. Using silence after a question, between comments, or in strategic locations helps to preserve the rational nature of a dialogue and diffuse the heat that can carry a conversation from a dialogue into a debate.

8. **Don't be defensive.** Not everyone will agree with the topic, the activities, or the company present, but it is important that you not take comments personally. You're doing the best you can; it is difficult to please everyone. Try not to let your speech or body language show that you have taken a dislike to someone in the group who seems to be a negative force.

9. **Be flexible** even while trying to keep the dialogue focused. If the group seems to want to pursue a diversion, allow some time to discuss the new

topic but bring the conversation back afterwards: "If I could interject, you all seem keen on talking about the terrible relations between campus security and the neighborhood. Let's go ahead and lay that issue on the table for 10 minutes and then get back to our topic of student activism in the community."

10. **Remember that you are a facilitator, not an expert.** A facilitator should not feel that she or he has to have answers to questions, know all of the facts, be able to cite references, or possess any of the other marks of authority often associated with group leadership. Your task is to bring out the best from the group, not to be the most articulate spokesperson.

AVOIDING PROBLEMS

Protecting participants from those who abuse the ground rules is an unpleasant but important part of the facilitator's job. You can minimize the likelihood that you will have to be a referee if you plan carefully, seek the right participants, lay out the ground rules clearly, and run a session in which participants generally respect one another. But when the topic for discussion is controversial or incites passion, managing the conversation can be tricky. The most common problems or conflicts that may need managing include people who:

- Talk too much
- Never talk
- Get off topic
- Are overly aggressive and always want to argue
- Attack other people rather than discuss the topic
- Use conversation as an ego boost
- Goof off or disrupt the conversation

As facilitator, you can use the following tools or approaches (adapted from the University of Kansas' Community Tool Box; see http://ctb.ku.edu/tools) for dealing with these problems, beginning with the least obtrusive and moving to the most direct and confrontational:

- **Use the unity of the group.** If you are successful at getting people to accept the ground rules, the group itself can help you in keeping the conversation on track, gently sidestepping issues, or diverting attention away from would-be troublemakers and bringing in shy participants. Recognize the peacemakers in the group and call on them if and when you need allies.

- **Use the agenda or ground rules** to manage individuals. Quietly remind the group of the topic if someone starts to move in an inappropriate direction. Remind a participant of the difference between a debate and a dialogue if you feel that his or her statements are too confrontational. Sometimes clarifying questions can soften confrontational comments: "You say that 'all politicians are crooks.' Can you describe some of the conditions that are forced on a person in politics that might make an honest person a little less honest?"

- **Be honest.** If you have established yourself as a person with the sincere interests of the group in mind, you may simply want to issue an honest statement: "We are getting off the subject here, and while the point you raise is an interesting one, I want to make the best use of our time to help us understand the stated topic."

- **Use humor.** If you are comfortable with the use of humor, you might try to make light of someone's abuse of ground rules: "Well, I guess you know a lot about this issue. Can we hear from someone who's less of an expert?" Be careful using humor, though, as it can be dangerous if you don't know the person or have not established the right rapport.

- **Accept a position but soften it.** Sometimes recognizing someone's extreme position may be used as a way of inviting other, less extreme points of view: "Joe, I hear you and your absolute objection to capital punishment. I wonder if someone can restate the objection in a way that leaves room for conversation with others who don't share Joe's conviction."

- **Take a break.** If none of the above techniques works to alter the behavior of a participant and the behavior continues to detract from or derail the dialogue, you might want to take a brief break and quietly ask the offender to restrain him- or herself or withdraw from the conversation for the good of the group. This step is seldom needed.

WRAPPING UP

The process of dialogue can be abstract, with many ideas and words but no clear-cut conclusion. The facilitator must summarize the flow of the conversation, suggest some of the lessons learned, and outline any next steps that might have emerged.

If student interest was high, you might spend a few minutes talking about other topics for discussion. Gauge interest in future dialogue, and if you feel comfortable doing so, ask for verbal feedback, which is often much more useful than written evaluation forms. Don't lose the energy that may exist at the end of a dialogue. Set a date and time for another dialogue and discuss ways to publicize the event. Participants may have unique audiences with which they want to share the news. Use the specific talents and enthusiasms of the group.

Evaluating the Dialogue

It is important to get feedback on the different issues that you discussed so that you can effectively summarize the effectiveness of your plans and prepare for future dialogues. You can modify the Dialogue Evaluation Form on the next page to fit your dialogue, or you can create your own form. If you would like participants' feedback on your facilitation efforts, see the Facilitator's Evaluation Form that follows. You can also use this form to review the different skills you will use as facilitator.

Dialogue Evaluation Form

Did you enjoy the dialogue?	Yes	No	Uncertain
Would you attend another, more focused dialogue?	Yes	No	Uncertain
Would you bring a friend?	Yes	No	Uncertain

Which topics would you like to spend more time discussing?

Other comments:

Would you be interested in becoming a
dialogue facilitator?   Yes   No

Can we contact you regarding future dialogues?   Yes   No

If yes, please provide your email address _____

Can you think of any other people—faculty, staff, students, or community members—on or around campus who we ought to include in future dialogues? If so, please list them below.

Name:_____ Phone:_____ Email:_____

Name:_____ Phone:_____ Email:_____

Name_____   Phone:_____ Email:_____

(An electronic copy of this form is available at www.actionforchange.org/dialogues/forms.html.)

Facilitator Evaluation Form

5 = Fully agree 1 = Do not agree at all

The facilitator(s) helped us to:

1. All participate in the discussion.   5 4 3 2 1
2. Promote mutual learning and understanding.   5 4 3 2 1
3. Foster inclusive solutions.   5 4 3 2 1
4. Use our time effectively.   5 4 3 2 1
5. Make good use of the information available to us.   5 4 3 2 1
6. Establish common objectives for the meeting.   5 4 3 2 1
7. Adhere to our meeting norms.   5 4 3 2 1
8. Remain clear about our tasks.   5 4 3 2 1
9. Clarify steps we would follow in performing our tasks.   5 4 3 2 1
10. Stay conscious of the processes that we were trying to use.   5 4 3 2 1
11. Get back on track when we were confused.   5 4 3 2 1
12. Keep our inputs relevant.   5 4 3 2 1
13. Keep our inputs clear.   5 4 3 2 1
14. Communicate respectfully with one another.   5 4 3 2 1
15. Develop sufficient information about all topics discussed.   5 4 3 2 1
16. Explore alternatives fully before making decisions.   5 4 3 2 1
17. Encourage differences in opinion.   5 4 3 2 1
18. Manage conflict.   5 4 3 2 1

The facilitator(s):

19. Listened actively.   5 4 3 2 1
20. Summarized and synthesized key points.   5 4 3 2 1
21. Asked open-ended questions.   5 4 3 2 1
22. Reserved judgment and kept an open mind.   5 4 3 2 1
23. Summarized and synthesized key points.   5 4 3 2 1
24. Encouraged people to take responsibility for their own actions.   5 4 3 2 1

Other constructive comments:

(An electronic copy of this form is available at www.actionforchange.org/dialogues/forms.html.)

Immediately after the dialogue, planners should review the highlights and the problems encountered in order to celebrate their success and capture first impressions of the lessons learned. Usually, it takes a while to understand the lessons that emerge. You and the others on the planning team should thoroughly analyze the dialogue by:

- Reviewing notes
- Listening to audiotapes
- Talking with participants privately
- Following up in small-group discussions
- Summarizing the session in writing

Creating a Follow-up Plan

Use the information you acquired during the dialogue, from the notes or tapes gathered during the session, and from the evaluation forms to think about next steps. You may decide that offering the same or a slightly modified dialogue to another group might clarify ideas or help you better understand how that group thinks about the same topic. Or you might decide to invite the same group back for a follow-up discussion of a topic that emerged from the first dialogue.

Do not limit these next steps only to more talk. While further dialogue may be the logical follow-up, some dialogues suggest a more active approach. As you think about the outcome of the dialogue, consider the range of actions available in a democratic society. These include:

- **Use information** by becoming informed and informing others (e.g., by organizing information campaigns or teach-ins).
- **Make contributions** of money, materials, or time (direct service).
- **Alter lifestyles** through economic boycotts, environmental behavior, or changing social patterns.
- **Use your voice** by voting, writing or calling representatives or media outlets, or petitioning.
- **Take an active stand**—either proactive or reactive—by serving as an advocate or campaigning for an issue, lobbying, publishing, running for office, or protesting.

Some dialogues lend themselves to follow-up activities more naturally than others. For example, a dialogue on the relationship between your campus and its neighbors might suggest that students engage in:

- A mapping activity to better understand existing relations between the college and the neighborhood (information).

- A campaign to collect contributions for needy families at Christmas (contributions).

- A boycott of a college bookstore that has undermined a local business (altering lifestyles).

- Creating a petition that calls for increased community voice in the campus's expansion plans (using voice).

- Researching and publishing a map of all campus-owned property in a neighborhood to demonstrate land-use issues (taking a proactive stand).

- Practicing civil disobedience on campus until concessions are made to neighbors in exchange for a new dorm being built in a residential neighborhood (taking a reactive stand).

In each scenario, it is important for dialogue organizers to work collaboratively with groups and individuals on campus to ensure adequate support for any initiatives. While a strong agenda may emerge from a dialogue of 15 students, the success of any action will hinge on the extent to which that action has a solid base of support.

It is also critical to think about the necessary and logical order of actions. True democracy follows the same principles as dialogues—listening to the voices of others with respect. It is unfair to protest an action before you understand the full complexity of an issue and have tried other, less confrontational approaches to resolving conflict.

Managing Public Relations

Once your dialogue is over, you will want to tell key people on campus more about the event. A major part of building a spirit of civic engagement on campus is to inform others that students are serious about world issues and want to make an impact. Getting your story in the campus newspaper will let administrators, faculty, staff members, and other students know that students are interested in more than last weekend's football game or the latest movie review. Using the press to try to shape campus culture is a major civic act.

As with publicizing the event beforehand, one option is to prepare a press release (see the sample that follows, adapted from an actual press release for one of the pilot dialogues held in 2002). You should also contact the school paper to discuss the civic engagement project and the dialogue (it may be helpful to be able to provide photos). Another option is to send a brief letter to your college or university president telling her or him of the basic ideas that emerged from the meeting and perhaps copying other key administrators on campus to inform the campus community of the form, function, and outcome of the dialogues.

Sample Post-Dialogue Press Release

FOR IMMEDIATE RELEASE

Contact: [include contact information here]

May 30, 2002

California College Students Field-Test National Civic Initiative

California State University Los Angeles—On Friday, May 29, a dozen students met for a dialogue on student involvement in public life at the EPIC center on campus. This was the first of a series of similar dialogues that are being hosted on campuses across the country as part of a civic engagement initiative sponsored by Campus Compact and funded by The Pew Charitable Trusts. Cal State LA and the EPIC Center were selected for this field-testing because campus students have been involved in community service for more than 35 years.

Students who attended the dialogue were eager to learn how other students are engaged and to see their community service within the larger context of addressing social and economic problems through service and political action. One student summarized the feelings of many in the group when he stated, "Before I became involved in community service, all I wanted was to get my degree and go out and earn money. Now I plan to go back into my community after I graduate and work with other community members to solve some of the problems my community faces."

This is the first in a series of dialogues designed to get students talking about their work in communities and to explore additional civic strategies. Students also began to assess the role of the university in supporting (or hindering) civic work by students. More information about student-led dialogues can be found at www.compact.org. Information on EPIC can be found at http://instructional1.calstatela.edu/EPIC.

Sample Civic Dialogues

The following sections present some sample dialogues as models for you to follow closely, loosely, or not at all. They represent a wide variety of different dialogue topics and styles. We have tried to represent some of the ways you may begin this process on your own campus.

Do not expect your dialogues to follow the exact path that these examples take. Your dialogues will grow dynamically depending on the participants; trying to make them fit into a mold will only repress free-flowing discussion. These examples should be seen only as guides. For easy reference, the topics they address are listed here:

- Sample Dialogue 3-1: Students and the Public Good
- Sample Dialogue 3-2: What Is Civic Engagement?
- Sample Dialogue 3-3: Hunger and Homelessness
- Sample Dialogue 3-4: Why Be Patriotic?
- Sample Dialogue 3-5: Understanding September 11
- Sample Dialogue 3-6: Civic Action: The Legacy of Cesar E. Chavez
- Sample Dialogue 3-7: Students Creating Engaged Campuses
- Sample Dialogue 3-8: Is Your Service Democratic?

Additional sample dialogues exploring the connections between service and politics appear in Chapter 4.

Sample Dialogue 3-1: Students and the Public Good

This sample includes several activities or discussion points, each with a prompt to begin the conversation. Feel free to pick and choose among these activities or to create your own.

Goals: To introduce students to dialogues, explore the connection between service and activism, and discuss the support of the college for student public life.

Introduction: Set the context with some background information, such as:

> Students across the country are participating in discussions like this to better understand how students are involved in public life. By public life, we mean actions that people take to address the quality of life of others beyond their immediate circle of family or friends. To some, it might mean tutoring a child, protesting for living wages of employees on campus, or creating a socially responsible investing option with university endowments.
>
> The purpose of this dialogue is not to argue those causes, although we will attempt to identify them. What we hope to understand is how and why you are

drawn to what we will refer to as civic engagement and how you see that work having an effect. We will also spend some time talking about how the campus supports or hinders you in the work you have chosen to be involved in and what it might do to be more supportive.

Activity 1—Personal narratives: You may want to conduct this session as a "Quaker dialogue" in which you go around the circle and give each participant a chance to briefly tell her or his story with no questions or comments. Those not willing to speak or wanting a bit more time can simply pass. Explain that you wish to leave a few seconds of silence after each speaker to give people a chance to reflect briefly on what they have heard. You might begin to model the response and give participants more time to think about their response.

Prompt: As the facilitator, you might say something like: "After giving us your name, year in school, and major, please tell us which of these selections from the handout best represents your attitude toward public life. [See the handout, Perspectives on Civic Engagement, in the sidebar that follows.] In what ways did you agree with the narratives and in which ways did you disagree? Use examples from your own life that tell us a bit more about your position. If you think none of these stories represents your position, describe your views as clearly and briefly as possible."

Activity 2—Listing critical issues: The simplest way of conducting this activity is to have participants list the public issues that they have found most engaging, without asking for the details of their involvement. You may want to invite clarifying questions that help participants better understand the issues or problem. For example, if someone offers an issue like "language," a brief conversation may be necessary to understand language as a public issue.

Prompt: "In listening to the kinds of issues you are involved with, we can begin to make a list of what you believe to be critical. Let's add to that list. What public issues do you feel most strongly about and invest time in attempting to address? In what ways do you go about addressing these issues?"

Activity 3—Solving problems in the public domain: You may want to take an issue that seems to engage several different participants, perhaps involved in different ways, and focus initially on that issue. Education is frequently a good choice. Let students describe how they see their own work addressing the problem and allow a free-flowing conversation, attempting to ensure that people respect one another's position and that everyone who wants to speak can do so.

Prompt: "How do see your own work on these issues contributing to a solution to problems?"

Handout for Dialogue 3-1: Perspectives on Civic Engagement

There are many different positions on involvement in public life, ranging from noninvolvement to those who would radically change the very nature of our social, political, or economic structures. The purpose of using the following narratives is not to see the full range of student engagement but only to get the conversation started. As you read these descriptions, try to identify which comes closest to capturing your attitude or position about engagement in public life. If none of them do, think of how you would briefly capture your position. [Read each narrative below without comment.]

Donald: "I grew up poor, so I know all about the problems and causes firsthand. My contribution to public life is to do well in school, get a job, eventually own my own business, hire others, pay taxes, and buy a lot of goods and services. I think I can do good by doing well and leave the social causes to the do-gooders and the politics to the politicians."

Tran: "I think students are like apprentices in a democracy. We are learning to become effective citizens. While I don't think my work helping as a tutor to two third-grade boys will change the world, I think it is helping Miguel and Ricky. At the same time, it is teaching me a lot about things like urban education, the issues immigrant children face, and the web of problems families must deal with in poor communities. I think that knowledge will help me be a more effective citizen in the future."

Shawna: "There have always been problems; there will always be problems. I don't feel that I can get the truth from the biased press. I know I can't trust the politicians. The government is only out for my money no matter who is in office. I have no interest in public life. I don't think my participation is important and have better things to do with my time."

Marcia: "I have been very involved in working with local unions and their battles with local employers including the college. Until we address some of the basic economic inequalities in society, the problems associated with poverty will continue. Currently I am working to get Yolanda Brown elected as our congressional representative. Yolanda is pro-labor and will be a strong voice in Washington for better working conditions and fair pay."

Jeremy: "Last year I began working at a homeless shelter and soup kitchen in my community. Working with the people in the shelter exposed me to a long list of reasons why people become homeless. One main reason is the housing crisis in our city. Housing is not affordable for many people, even those who work. My work at the shelter motivated me to get involved in an affordable housing campaign with a community group committed to ending homelessness. I have called the governor and other elected officials and attended numerous protests at the State House. I have also become involved with a group fighting for a living wage for maintenance workers at my university. I have actually seen some of these cleaners and their families eating at the soup kitchen."

Activity 4—Exploring service and politics: This question focuses on the connection, if any, between service to the community and political action. Again, at least initially, you may wish to return to the Quaker dialogue format for this discussion to ensure that every voice is heard again. After phrasing the question, give everyone a few seconds to frame his or her answer before beginning. After hearing from everyone, open the discussion for deeper dialogue.

Prompt: "Many in our society are concerned that students are disengaged from civic issues because we do not vote in large numbers and are not very involved in traditional political campaigns. What connection, if any, do you see between the service that you do and traditional ideas of politics such as voting, campaigning, and letter writing? Do you believe that voting and other forms of political participation are effective ways of addressing public issues?"

Activity 5—Discussing the role of higher education: A discussion of the role of higher education in civic engagement is probably best structured as free and open, with someone capturing thoughts on flip-chart paper or a chalkboard so that participants can build on ideas already offered. You may wish to write people's comments in two columns, "Help" and "Hinder."

Prompt: "How does your college or university help support student civic engagement and foster student voice on your campus? How does the college or university hinder student civic engagement and stifle student voice on your campus?" You may then ask a follow-up question, such as, "If you wanted to make a change on campus, how would you go about doing so?"

Wrap-up and action: Summarize the flow of conversation and the major points, and note that you will contact participants after you and your organizing team have reflected on the dialogue. Hand out an evaluation form and express your appreciation for the group's time and attention. Analyze the comments from students and think about how to best summarize the students' work and their perceptions for campus administrators. Or focus on one obstacle that students identified in common and meet with administrators to examine the problem.

Sample Dialogue 3-2: What Is Civic Engagement?

Goal: To discuss ways of defining civic engagement individually and as a group.

Introduction: As facilitator, give some background information, such as:

> The Raise Your Voice Campaign aims to increase civic engagement among America's young people. This raises the initial question, What is civic engagement? Here are definitions from various sources:

> Project 540 [www.project540.org] says that civic engagement consists of adding one's voice to community conversations; advocating on behalf of others; partici-

pating in public life; encouraging other people to participate in public life; and joining in common work that promotes the well-being of everyone.

The Pew Charitable Trusts [www.pewtrusts.org] defines civic engagement as "Individual and collective actions designed to identify and address issues of public concern," and goes on to note that "Civic engagement can take many forms, from individual volunteerism to organizational involvement to electoral participation. It can include efforts to directly address an issue, work with others in a community to solve a problem or interact with the institutions of representative democracy."

A definition from Raise Your Voice student reads, in part, "Engagement is more than just volunteering, although volunteering can be engagement. Engagement is more than just voting, although voting can be engagement. Engagement is a combination of voice, action, and reflection. Engagement exists when individuals recognize that they have responsibilities not only to themselves and their families, but also to their communities—local, national, and global."

Of course, these are general definitions. Each of you may associate different actions and ideas with the words civic engagement.

Activity—Defining engagement: This exercise is useful as an opening dialogue to capture the different ways people view civic engagement. Ask participants how they define civic engagement. You may want to use a worksheet listing actions that might be considered civic and have participants spend 10 minutes numbering each item from 1–15 according to how closely it fits her or his definition of civic engagement. (See the handout on the next page, titled How Do You Define Civic Engagement?)

After participants have completed filling out their sheets individually, have them get together in groups of two to four to share their first and last choices. Have them discuss why they ranked their choices as they did (15 minutes).

Reassemble participants for whole-group discussion and ask the following questions (20 minutes):

- What were the differences among students in your group?
- Were certain items ranked high by all students in the group? Why? Were certain items ranked low? Why?
- What did you learn from each other about the reasons some actions were ranked as they were?
- What did this exercise teach you about people's ideas concerning participation in civic life?
- Does a "continuum of engagement" exist? What are the underlying criteria for such a continuum?

Handout for Dialogue 3-2: How Do You Define Civic Engagement?

People define civic engagement in many different ways. Represented below are items that people might cite as examples of civic engagement. Place a "1" next to the action that most closely models your own idea of civic engagement. Place a "2" next to the action that is the second closest, etc., up to 15.

_____ Joining the armed forces.

_____ Helping to start an after-school program for children in an underprivileged neighborhood.

_____ Talking with a friend about social issues.

_____ Working for a candidate in a local or national election.

_____ Serving on a jury.

_____ Protesting at a local corporation that has a plant overseas employing child workers.

_____ Giving to the United Way.

_____ Biking or walking to work or school every day.

_____ Tutoring an adult literacy student.

_____ Attending a neighborhood meeting.

_____ Serving dinner once a week at a soup kitchen.

_____ Writing to legislators about an issue of importance to you.

_____ Giving blood.

_____ Stopping to assist a driver whose car has broken down on the side of the road.

_____ Voting.

(Adapted from "How Do You Define Service," an exercise created by Kent Koth and Scott Hamilton, 1993. Used by permission.)

Wrap-up and action: Use this activity to initiate a "notch it up" campaign in which students take an online quiz that is used to develop their own continuum of engagement, then to place themselves on that continuum to see what actions might be important for them to consider as more engaged students.

Sample Dialogue 3-3: Hunger and Homelessness

This dialogue was developed in partnership with the National Student Campaign Against Hunger and Homelessness for use during Hunger and Homelessness Week in November.

Goal: To discuss the root causes of hunger and homelessness and how these issues have affected, and will continue to affect, students' lives.

Introduction: As facilitator, present some statistics on hunger and homelessness to the group. (Statistics can be found at www.nscahh.org.) Read the following quote, which is often used to highlight the potential shortfall of direct service with solely a charity orientation:

> Doing service as a college student was such a meaningful experience for me. I hope that my children have the opportunity to do service in homeless shelters someday.

After reading the quote, have the group brainstorm about the benefits of direct service in homeless shelters and the possible negative consequences of the direct service approach. In the following discussions, suggest that the group think about what the implications are of assuming that there will be homeless shelters for our children to work in, and to imagine what society would look like if there weren't. What are the root causes for homeless shelters and soup kitchens, and how can we work to deepen our service to address the immediate needs of these shelters, while working constantly toward the long-term goal of ending the need for such shelters?

Activity 1—Outcomes of direct service: Ask the entire group this question: What are the positive and negative outcomes of direct service by college students at homeless shelters? List their comments in two columns on a chalkboard or flip-chart paper.

Activity 2—Awareness and accomplishment: Have the group break into smaller groups of four to five people to discuss the quote, focusing on the following questions:

- How can you connect direct service with public policy changes that will make it less likely hunger and homelessness will exist in 20 years?

- What are the homeless and hunger issues facing the people in the communities surrounding your campus? Do you know people working for your college or university who are struggling with hunger or homelessness?

- What groups in your community or on your campus are working to address these issues? What different methods are they using? What have been some successes, and some struggles?

- What specific actions can you take on your campus to promote awareness of hunger and homelessness?

Wrap-up and action: Report on the small groups' ideas and write them on flipchart paper. Ask if participants are interested in following up on some of the ideas and use the momentum of the conversation to implement an action plan.

Sample Dialogue 3-4: Why Be Patriotic?

Goal: To examine what it means to be patriotic and whether citizens owe anything to their country.

Introduction: As facilitator, give participants some background information, such as:

> Since September 11, 2001, there has been a remarkable surge in patriotic sentiment. Flags hang from many offices, homes, and cars, and the U.S. media have been flooded with stories celebrating all things American. Everyone from politicians to next-door neighbors seems to be loudly proclaiming their patriotism, but all seem to have a different definition of it and apply it in different ways.

> An AmeriCorps volunteer feels patriotic because he is teaching inner-city children how to read, while a soldier feels patriotic because he is serving in the Middle East. This conversation seeks to find out how college students define patriotism at this point in time and whether students think patriotism is an important value to possess.

Activity 1—Defining patriotism: Ask the group read a handout with quotes about patriotism (see the handout in the sidebar below), then split them up into pairs to develop their own definitions.

When the pairs seem ready, bring the group back together to share their definitions. Write them all on a chalkboard or easel; then try to get the group to synthesize them into one definition, even if it is long and wordy.

Activity 2—How important is patriotism? After a consensus is reached, have the group break into groups of four or five to discuss the following questions:

- Are you patriotic? Why or why not?

Handout for Dialogue 3-4: Statements about Patriotism

"Patriotism is a lively sense of collective responsibility."

—RICHARD ADLINGTON, BRITISH AUTHOR

"Patriotism is proud of a country's virtues and eager to correct its deficiencies; it also acknowledges the legitimate patriotism of other countries, with their own specific virtues. The pride of nationalism, however, trumpets its country's virtues and denies its deficiencies, while it is contemptuous toward the virtues of other countries. It wants to be, and proclaims itself to be, 'the greatest,' but greatness is not required of a country; only goodness is."

—SYDNEY J. HARRIS, U.S. JOURNALIST AND REVIEWER

"Johnson suddenly uttered, in a strong determined tone, an apothegm, at which many will start: 'Patriotism is the last refuge of a scoundrel.' But let it be considered that he did not mean a real and generous love of our country, but that pretended patriotism which so many, in all ages and countries, have made a cloak of self-interest."

—JAMES BOSWELL, SCOTTISH BIOGRAPHER, ON THE FAMOUS QUOTE FROM SAMUEL JOHNSON

"What do we mean by patriotism in the context of our times? I venture to suggest that what we mean is a sense of national responsibility ... a patriotism which is not short, frenzied outbursts of emotion, but the tranquil and steady dedication of a lifetime."

—ADLAI STEVENSON, U.S. STATESMAN

"Patriotism is when love of your own people comes first; nationalism, when hate for people other than your own comes first."

—CHARLES DE GAULLE, FRENCH GENERAL AND PRESIDENT

"The world is a fine place. The only thing wrong with it is us. How little justice and humility there is in us, how poorly we understand patriotism!"

—ANTON CHEKHOV, RUSSIAN AUTHOR AND PLAYWRIGHT

"I do not mean to exclude altogether the idea of patriotism. I know it exists, and I know it has done much in the present contest. But I will venture to assert, that a great and lasting war can never be supported on this principle alone. It must be aided by a prospect of interest, or some reward."

—GEORGE WASHINGTON, FIRST U.S. PRESIDENT

"You'll never have a quiet world until you knock the patriotism out of the human race."

—GEORGE BERNARD SHAW, ANGLO-IRISH PLAYWRIGHT AND CRITIC

"'My country, right or wrong' is a thing that no patriot would think of saying except in a desperate case. It is like saying 'My mother, drunk or sober.'"

—G.K. CHESTERTON, BRITISH AUTHOR AND THEOLOGIAN

"What is Americanism? Every one has a different answer. Some people say it is never to submit to the dictation of a King. Others say Americanism is the pride of liberty and the defense of an insult to the flag with their gore. When some half-developed person tramples on that flag, we should be ready to pour out the blood of the nation, they say. But do we not sit in silence when that flag waves over living conditions which should be an insult to all patriotism?"

—ANNE HOWARD SHAW, U.S. MINISTER AND SUFFRAGETTE

- What sort of patriotic behaviors do you see around you on campus?
- Should college students be patriotic? Should all citizens be patriotic?
- Does the country need patriotism?

Reassemble the participants and have each group report briefly what they discussed. Note that in his Call to Service, President George W. Bush asked Americans to donate 4,000 hours (two years) of community service over their lifetimes because "America needs men and women who respond to the call of duty, who stand up for the weak, who speak up for their beliefs, who sacrifice for a greater good" (Ohio State University commencement address, June 14, 2002). As a capstone to the dialogue, have the whole group discuss the following questions:

- Do you owe anything to your country? If so, what?
- Do you identify with the Call to Service, military service, or another form of national service?
- Do you see a connection between patriotism and service?

Wrap-up and action: Based on the information and understanding developed through this dialogue, work with the student newspaper to initiate a "Patriots in Action" series focusing on the work of different students and alumni that underscores the many different understandings of the word *patriot*.

Sample Dialogue 3-5: Understanding September 11

Goal: To have a dialogue on the terrorist attack on America in order to reflect on the context for the attack. It may be most appropriate to hold such a dialogue near the anniversary of the attack.

Introduction: As the facilitator, read aloud or distribute copies of a handout discussing the terrorist attack for participants to read (see the sidebar that follows on Understanding 9/11).

Activity 1—Exploring individuals' understanding: On 3 x 5 inch index cards, have each participant quickly write down what he or she believe are the reasons for the terrorist attacks on America; the cards are not collected but are used for the discussion. Lead a modified Quaker dialogue in which each participant briefly describes her or his understanding of the causes of the attack. Each person's comments are followed by a brief silence so that everyone can think about what was said and jot down a word or two that summarizes the points on the back of his or her card. This gives everyone a chance to speak.

Activity 2—Sharing and revising responses: After everyone has spoken, open the dialogue. It is important for the group to be respectful of other positions and to

Handout for Dialogue 3-5: Understanding 9/11

> "Should I have kept my views to myself until I learned all the facts? I don't believe so. Had I not acquired the habit of voicing my beliefs, I might never have taken a stand for or against the [Vietnam] war. The lesson I learned...was the importance of remaining open to other points of view and letting new arguments, information, and perspectives change my mind.... Sometimes those who oppose us have the most to teach us.
>
> —PAUL ROGAT LOEB,
> *SOUL OF A CITIZEN: LIVING WITH CONVICTION IN A CYNICAL TIME,* P. 52

September 11, 2001, was a terrible and traumatic day for our nation. It will define us for years to come and may be one of the defining moments of our history. In these days of commemoration, it is also important for us to try to understand the events of that day and their aftermath. It is far to easy too recall the smashing of fast-flying planes into buildings that seemed like they would stand forever; to recall the fires, the falling bodies, the disintegration of monuments that celebrated America's economic well-being and its capacity to challenge the very law of gravity. Most likely, all of us can remember where we were as we watched the panic that struck the streets of New York and the major cities of the country.

To many people, these images have become our understanding of September 11. But the images only represent one moment in time. As part of our remembrance, it is important for us to consider all that led up to September 11, and all that has happened since.

What do we know and understand about the causes and effects of the terrorist attack on America? How do we understand the anger it would take for 20 men to live in secret in a society they hated and then give up their lives for a symbolic act? Do men like this hope to win a war through terror, or only hope that terror itself can destroy from within, like some terrible cancer upon the nation? What do we know about the world stage, the meaning of the symbols chosen for targets, the history of relations between the United States and the Middle East, where this hatred of America was born and fostered?

Now, while the fear subsides, are we attempting to understand the new American foreign policy that has emerged post–September 11? Do we question the host of almost invisible changes in our democratic system? Have we become too willing to exchange our heritage of rights and freedoms for what we hope will be increased security? Do we seek to understand the costs of these decisions on the economic health of the nation?

After September 11, there was a flurry of book buying, campus teach-ins, and public forums as people sought understanding of these complex issues, but many soon retreated from inquiry for fear of sounding unpatriotic. The message of patriotism was not subtle or inferred. Not long after the military action against Afghanistan began, White House Press Secretary Ari Fleischer warned that Americans "need to watch what they say." The president announced, "You are either for us or against us." What are we left to understand, and how are we to express it?

As Paul Loeb says in *Soul of a Citizen,* we have an obligation as citizens to take an informed stand, right or wrong. We need to voice and defend our position as we understand it now—and then we need to fill in additional facts, listen to others, and be diligent in our search for understanding. We either undertake our civic responsibility to understand history or become prisoners to someone else's version of the truth.

The activity you are about to engage in is designed to help you in this process. Don't worry if you feel that you do not "know" the answer. As Socrates stated, "the only true wisdom is in knowing you know nothing." Please share your beliefs about the causes of September 11 as well as you can, if for no other reason than to mark your beginning in the journey toward understanding.

seek middle ground. As Paul Loeb would remind us, the person who wishes to learn the truth must remain "open to other points of view and letting new arguments, information, and perspectives" change his or her mind.

Capture the underlying themes, points of unresolved differences, and questions raised during the course of the dialogue. Summarize the session by underscoring areas of agreement, highlighting critical areas of disagreement, and reviewing the questions that arose.

On a second 3 x 5 inch card, have each participant briefly revise his or her original statement. Ask participants who indicated at the beginning of the dialogue that they had no idea what causes led to the attack to respond to the question, "Which positions that you have heard today sound most reasonable to you?" This gives them the last word and an opportunity to voice their views.

Wrap-up and action: In concluding, quickly review the different positions or causes that have been recorded and indicate that the full story of September 11 will take years to reveal. Point out that as scholars and citizens, students have an obligation to continue working to understand this historic event to the best of their ability.

Sample Dialogue 3-6: Civic Action—The Legacy of Cesar E. Chavez

This dialogue was developed by Julie C. Rodriguez of the Cesar E. Chavez Foundation.

Goals: To introduce students to forums for exchanging ideas, exploring the connection between service and activism, and discussing the support of colleges and universities for student public life.

Introduction: As facilitator, give some background information about student activism, such as: "Student movements have been at the forefront of some historic changes in our country. Students helped to mobilize people during the Civil Rights and Chicano Movements." If possible, add some examples from your state: "In California, students spread the word about the injustices taking place in the fields and took to the streets to oppose the anti-immigrant and anti-affirmative action propositions (Prop. 187 and 209), among others." Follow with an overview of what you hope to explore: "What motivates young people to get involved in their communities? What does youth involvement look like? There are many ways young people can and should be involved in their communities."

Then ask those present to introduce themselves and state what brought them to the conversation. If no one volunteers to go first, you can start things off; introduce yourself by stating your name, year, and major, followed by a statement such as, "I came to this discussion today to begin to think about and work toward building a stronger network of students who want to make a difference here on campus and in the community."

Next briefly introduce the life and work of Cesar Chavez, which centered on civic action, civic engagement, and civic responsibility. You may want to prompt, "How many of you know who Cesar Chavez was?" Then provide an explanation such as the following. (At the end, you may want to add a personal anecdote about how Chavez inspired you or someone you know.)

> Chavez was a migrant farm worker who believed in social justice for all people, so he set out to organize and empower people to help themselves. He's most widely know for co-founding the first successful farm-worker union in U.S. history, the United Farm Workers of America, but his struggle and ideals transcend any one movement or cause. During the 1950s, he worked for the Community Service Organization promoting civic participation in barrios and communities throughout California. He was a strong proponent of nonviolent social action and helped to bring about monumental changes in the lives of farm workers and all working people across the United States. Under Chavez's leadership, the farm worker movement changed the face of American society by empowering one of the poorest, least educated sectors of our country.

Activity 1—What will make the difference? Read or write (large enough for all to see) the following quote from Cesar Chavez, and ask participants to respond: "I've always maintained that it isn't the form that's going to make the difference. It isn't the rule or the procedure or the ideology, but it's human beings that will make it."

You may want to conduct this session as a Quaker dialogue in which you go around the circle and give everyone a chance to briefly explain their reaction to the quote with no questions or comments. Those not willing to speak or wanting a bit more time can simply pass. Explain that you wish to leave a few seconds of silence after each speaker to give people a chance to reflect briefly on what they have heard.

Prompt: "What are your reactions to this quote? In what ways do you agree with Cesar's statement? In what ways do you disagree?" As facilitator, you may want to go first to model the response and give participants a bit more opportunity to think through how they want to respond.

Recap: After people answer, recap some of the major points they made about the quote. Some reactions may include, "The power of people is the most powerful vehicle for social change." "Politicians can't change society alone." "We need to hold our politicians accountable to the needs of the community." "It is our obligation and responsibility to be active in our communities."

Activity 2—Making a difference in the community: Next ask participants to discuss what making a difference in the community means to them. You can either continue in the Quaker dialogue mode if it is working for the group, or break into small groups to allow for a more free-flowing discussion, ensuring that all participants respect each other's views and have the opportunity to be fully heard before someone else is allowed to comment. Capture ideas and opinions on a flip-chart or chalkboard to allow participants to fully digest and reflect on what is being said. If you're using small groups, make sure each group has someone responsible for recording ideas.

Prompt: "In the quote, Chavez mentions that it is human beings who will make a difference in our world, not ideologies, rules, or procedures. What does it mean to you to make a difference in your life, your community, and the world? When you think of an ideal community, what do you envision?" If necessary, remind participants that they are there to listen to and respect one another's ideas and viewpoints, not to develop a consensus, and ask them to refrain from editorializing about others' responses.

Recap: With the whole group, review some of the major points participants made. Some reactions may include, "To make a difference in the community means to work with others to better their lives and my own." "To make a difference means to empower young people into action." "To make a difference means to work with others to get a quality education." "To make a difference means to work toward peace and justice."

Activity 3—What can we do? Have participants brainstorm specific ways to make a difference in the community. Break into small groups to allow for a more free-flowing discussion and brainstorming session, making sure each group has a recorder. You may want to divide the group by interest—for example, politics, education, campus-community issues, artistic expression (art, music, etc.) as a means of advocating for social change. Query the group to make sure you haven't missed any major interest groups.

When the larger group reassembles, have each of the smaller groups present their ideas for making a difference in the community. Record ideas on flip-chart paper or a chalkboard to allow participants to fully digest and reflect on each idea.

Prompt: "Let's take about 15 to 20 minutes to brainstorm ideas about how we can use what we're already interested in doing to make a difference in our communities. Each group should try to develop two or three ideas to share with larger group. If you want to combine some of the smaller groups for a more dynamic discussion, we can do that too."

Wrap-up and action: Review the ideas briefly and ask students to think about how to combine some of the ideas so they support one another. If there are still a lot of ideas on the board, talk to participants about what they think is a good first step for taking action. Ask participants if they would be willing to attend a follow-up meeting to develop an action plan and try to schedule a meeting date. Ask whether they are willing to contact other organizations on campus or in the community to invite them to join the discussions; request that everyone bring at least one other person to the next meeting.

Sample Dialogue 3-7: Students Creating Engaged Campuses

Goal: To discuss the role of higher education in community life and identify the barriers and main allies to civic engagement efforts on campus. Participants will evaluate their relative ability to influence campus engagement and consider points of access and power available to them.

Activity 1—Bolsters and barriers to engagement: As facilitator, ask people to turn to someone they do not know, introduce themselves (name, campus, etc.), and share one image or idea that fosters the creation of an engaged campus and one barrier. Give people five minutes to talk in pairs. If there are fewer than 20 people in the group, get names and record one brief item that the pairs discussed. If the group is larger, record several aids and barriers to engagement.

Activity 2—What is an engaged campus? Build on the warm-up activity by asking participants to write down the images, ideas, and elements that come to mind when they hear the words *engaged campus*. Ask people to share their responses; record them and discuss as a group. Then specifically ask participants to think about the roles of students, faculty, community organizations, and administrators. Challenge the group to think about the question: Is the extent of a campus's engagement determined only by the student civic engagement that is going on? Refer participants to a handout on How Students Are Creating an Engaged Campus (see the sidebar on p. 98); you may also want to share students' vision from the "Lessons Learned" declaration (in Chapter 1 of this book).

Have the group think about the following questions:

- Which ideas about an engaged campus do you agree with? Which ideas do you not agree with?
- What role do students play on your campus in building an engaged campus?
- Is there anything missing from the handout? Is bringing these actions together under an engaged campus framework helpful?

Activity 3—Overcoming barriers: Break participants into groups of three or four, with each one working on a challenge or barrier that was identified at the beginning. Make sure that everyone is in a group that he or she is interested in or that is relevant to his or her campus. Have them spend 10–15 minutes identifying the problem, the person or people responsible, those who may be able to fix the problem, and strategies students can take to address the situation. Ask them to write up their strategies and ideas on easel paper; give each group 2 minutes to present their strategies.

Wrap-up and action: Before breaking up, draw people's attention to the community mapping guide (see Chapter 2) as a tool for identifying key stakeholders on campus. You may want to assign groups to follow up by contacting relevant people on campus for help getting past the identified barrier. You may also want to schedule another meeting to review results and plan next steps.

Sample Dialogue 3-8: Is Your Service Democratic?

This dialogue is designed specifically for students who are engaged in service. Try to identify students from a range of service capacities.

Goal: To discuss the democratic dimensions and possibilities of community service with students engaged in different types of service.

Activity 1—How does service contribute to democracy? Begin by asking each participant to answer the questions in the handout (see the sidebar on Democratic Qualities of Service, on page 99).

Handout for Dialogue 3-7:
How Students Are Creating an Engaged Campus

Curriculum development and change. From Ethnic Studies to Service-Learning, students are using their power to advocate for an engaged curriculum that not only informs students about current public issues, but also facilitates their participation in community building and social change.

Creating structures to support student public work. Students have successfully advocated for programs and structures that help them act on public issues, such as a Civic Engagement Center, a Center for Peace & Justice, a Community Service Office, or a Service-Learning Center.

Public dialogue. On many campuses, students are looking for places where they can discuss a range of social issues. Students have often created such spaces, which range from town hall meetings to issues-oriented newspapers.

Institutional investment policies. By organizing to get their colleges to divest, students have encouraged their schools to invest funds directly in the local community or to pull investments from ventures they think are unethical (for example, the South African divestment movement). See "Investing in Social Change: Student Handbook on Community Investment by Colleges and Universities" at www.equitytrust.org/res_student.htm.

Purchasing policies or fair trade. Thousands of students have campaigned to encourage their campuses to use products made under fair, healthy labor conditions. United Students Against Sweatshops (www.usasnet.org) is a national student organization that fosters the manufacture of university apparel in safe, fair conditions. OXFAM America (www.oxfamamerica.org) supports student campaigns seeking to bring fair-trade coffee to campus.

Living wages. On many campuses, students are building efforts to develop a living wage policy that would ensure livable wages for all college or university employees (see www.campuslivingwage.org).

Food salvage, composting, and purchasing. Many student hunger and homelessness programs involve salvaging unused food from campus and taking it to appropriate community organizations. Efforts to support sustainable agriculture and local farmers have brought local and organic food to some campuses.

Energy efficient or sustainable campuses. At some colleges, students are figuring out how to make the physical presence of a campus less damaging to the environment and natural resources. Examples are student efforts to develop an entirely sustainable building or to create or expand recycling programs.

Handout for Dialogue 3-8: Democratic Qualities of Service

Please answer yes or no to the following questions:

_____ Does your service enhance public space and public institutions?

_____ Can you articulate the public significance of your service project?

_____ Does your service get others involved in community and public life?

_____ Does your service build on the capacities and strengths of members of the community where you are involved?

_____ Does your service help to build relationships between people in the community where you are involved?

_____ Does your service address the underlying causes to the problems you confront?

_____ Is your service visible?

_____ Does your service enable you and others to develop civic skills and talents?

_____ Do you have the opportunity to see your service through to a successful conclusion?

_____ Do all the people involved in the service project (service participants, community leaders, those served, others) decide together what is to be accomplished? Do they all engage in planning and designing the project?

_____ Are ongoing decisions made collectively? Are all the people involved in the service project accountable for the success or failure of the endeavor?

_____ Are all the people involved in the evaluation process and given an opportunity to raise questions about the process?

SCORE

8 or more "yes" responses—Your service project reflects the values and attributes of a thriving democracy.

4 to 7 "yes" responses—Good work, but more needs to be done to nurture democratic practices in your service work.

Fewer than 3 "yes" responses—Sometimes service benefits the one providing the service at the expense of others. Think carefully about how your work could be more democratic.

(Adapted from "Building Citizens: A Critical Reflection and Discussion Guide," Walt Whitman Center for the Culture and Politics of Democracy.)

Activity 2—Discussion: Once everyone is done with the test, add up the scores and then discuss how each item is important to the promotion of democracy. You may also open the discussion to different points of view on what other qualities may make a particular type of service democratic.

Dialogues in Action

As part of the Raise Your Voice campaign, tens of thousands of students on hundreds of campuses nationwide have held dialogues on topics of importance to them. In many cases, these dialogues have led to concrete actions such as the creation of a new program, a commitment to fair-trade purchasing, or even a visit to the state house. In other cases, the goal is to simply increase understanding of an issue. Following are a few examples to give you an idea of how campuses put the idea of dialogues to work.

HUMBOLDT STATE UNIVERSITY (CA)

Humboldt State University's Service Learning Center and Arcata High School's Students Against Violence Everywhere (SAVE) club hosted a forum open to all campus and community members who wanted to participate in an educated, respectful dialogue about campaign issues associated with the many referendum issues in the 2004 election.

OKLAHOMA STATE UNIVERSITY

An Oklahoma State University student and a professor trying to establish one of the first service-learning classes on campus hosted a dialogue between students and local veterans to educate students about recent wars and veterans' issues. At the dialogue, veterans from World War II, the Korean War, the Vietnam War, and the first Persian Gulf War conducted a panel presentation entitled "Veteran's Voice." After a public presentation, each of the veterans met in small groups with the more than 200 students in attendance to discuss the reality of war, along with the meaning of patriotism and heroism.

NORTH SHORE COMMUNITY COLLEGE (MA)

North Shore Community College hosted a homelessness forum, "It Isn't Going to Be Solved with a Clothing Drive," to discuss what college students can do to end homelessness. The forum brought together more than 250 students, community members, and state leaders focused on ending homelessness. As a result of the forum, the college assembled a working group to continue to seek solutions for affordable housing in the Lynn, Massachusetts, area.

MISSOURI CAMPUSES

Raise Your Voice and Missouri Campus Compact sponsored a student-led dialogue at the Missouri state capitol with hundreds of college students along with their legislators and the lieutenant governor. The dialogues focused on two questions: "What civic issues are important to students?" and "What are students doing to address these concerns?" Students reported on their dialogues on the floor of the state house.

MONTANA STATE UNIVERSITY–BILLINGS

Students sought to answer the question, "Whose responsibility is it?," sparked by large photographs depicting controversial subjects (famine and hunger, military torture, environmental degradation) in high-traffic areas around the campus. On large sheets of butcher paper hanging next to the photos, students wrote who they felt was responsible. Student leaders, along with faculty members, then led campus dialogues on the issues.

MADONNA UNIVERSITY (MI)

The Office of Multicultural Affairs hosted a one-night activity promoting intercultural dialogue among students, staff, and faculty during Black History Month. A cultural and artistic performance highlighted the contributions of different communities in the African Diaspora and their impact on U.S. society, followed by a discussion forum titled "Current Diversity Issues in Metro Detroit: Is It Only a Black/White Thing?" Students then explored how the current growth in diversity forces society to look at issues of race and ethnicity in nontraditional ways.

LAWRENCE UNIVERSITY (WI)

Students and community members gathered with Wisconsin Lieutenant Governor Barbara Lawton and local public officials to discuss "women in politics." As part of the discussion, the local Brown County Executive and the former Mayor of Seymour (now a Brown County board member) discussed their own experiences.

OBERLIN COLLEGE (OH)

The college hosted a forum on "The Fate and Future of Affirmative Action" at which President Nancy Dye, the Dean of Admissions, the Dean of the College of Arts and Sciences, and various professors discussed with students and community members their questions and concerns about affirmative action.

INDIANA UNIVERSITY–EAST

Students had lunch with Richmond Mayor Shelly Miller and County Councilman Ken Paust to discuss public service, the state of politics, and the importance of student involvement.

UNIVERSITY OF MAINE AT AUGUSTA

Students from various backgrounds participated in a forum on racial and ethnic tensions. Participants addressed issues such as the concept of "Americanism," the role diversity plays in the concept, and how students can make a difference in a silent majority.

UNIVERSITY OF NORTH TEXAS
A student team partnered with the North Texas Debate Program to host a student discussion of capital punishment policy in the state of Texas.

UNIVERSITY OF SAN DIEGO (CA)
Students hosted activist and educator Angela Davis, who spoke on campus, and then held a Civic Engagement Fair to highlight ways for students to get involved locally, highlight their work, and provide information on current issues. Community partners and students represented organizations such as Students for Life, the International Rescue Committee, the Center for Policy Initiatives, the National Lawyers Guild, the Islamic Leader Society, and the Republican Law Society.

Additional Resources on Dialogues

AmericaSpeaks, www.americaspeaks.org

Campus in Community, www.campusincommunity.org

Deliberative Democracy Consortium, www.deliberative-democracy.net

The Harwood Institute, www.theharwoodinstitute.org

Institute for Multi-Track Diplomacy, www.imtd.org

National Civic League, www.ncl.org

National Coalition for Dialogue and Deliberation, www.thataway.org

National Conference for Community and Justice, www.nccj.org

National Issues Forum, www.nifi.org

Study Circles Resource Center, www.studycircles.org

University of Colorado Conflict Research Consortium, www.colorado.edu/conflict/transform

The World Café, www.theworldcafe.com

References

Cortés, E., Jr. (1994, June/September). Reweaving the social fabric. *Boston Review*. (Available at www.bostonreview.net/BR19.3/Cortes.html.)

Loeb, P.R. (1999). *Soul of a citizen: Living with conviction in a cynical time.* New York: St. Martin's Griffin.

Wheatley, M.J. (2002, July/August). Some friends and I started talking...? All social change begins with a conversation. *Utne,* 112.

Chapter 4
Connecting Service and Political Engagement

In this chapter, we explore some common strategies for extending and deepening student engagement. What these strategies share is the same sort of deliberative process we introduced earlier in the book. Rethinking the role of service helps students build on existing service efforts while reconsidering the effects of such service on the deeper issues of systemic problems and political efforts to bring about change. To that end, we offer several sample dialogues and activities that students can use to continue the conversation on the connections between service and political engagement on campus.

We also provide practical models for connecting service with politics through means such as civic alternative spring break trips, pioneered by college students from Maine Campus Compact and Campus Compact for New Hampshire; communicating with legislators; alternative forms of political action; and visits to state capitols. Finally, we provide examples of campuses that have created hubs for civic engagement and service politics on campus.

Service Politics

Over the past decade, there has been widespread discussion of the connection—or, conversely, the lack of connection—between community service and politics. Many thoughtful and well-informed policy experts, armed with data on decreasing political involvement, have warned that college students are choosing community service as an alternative to political engagement. This opting out of the political process, they argue, is dangerous to the very foundation of American democracy. (See the statistics on service and voting in this book's Introduction.)

"The great reforming generations are the ones that marry the aspirations of service to the possibilities of politics and harness the good work done in local communities to transform a nation."

—E.J DIONNE (2000)

In response, Campus Compact convened a group of student leaders to discuss the connections between service and politics and their broader civic experiences on their

> "*Social critics from movements past will scratch their heads as we unite for political prisoners on Monday, indigenous persons on Tuesday, workers' rights on Wednesday, and spend the rest of the week quietly reading to grade school kids.... Service is a small hammer. By itself it can send small chips flying. Politics is like a chisel. To its own end, it can gouge the perfect surface. Together, with our hard work and inspiration, the hammer and chisel begin to carve something new, less perfect, and more human.*"
>
> —FABRICIO RODRIGUEZ, STUDENT ACTIVIST, IN THE NEW STUDENT POLITICS (LONG, 2002, P. II)

own terms and in their own language. The results of this 2001 meeting, the Wingspread Summit on Student Civic Engagement (see Chapter 1 for details), were both illuminating and controversial. In the seminal student-written publication that emerged from the conversation, *The New Student Politics: The Wingspread Statement on Student Civic Engagement*, students declared that their community service was not an "alternative to politics," but rather an "alternative politics."

An important conclusion was that, "This statement is not intended to be the final word on student engagement." Instead, it was meant to open a conversation on the connections between service and politics for other students on campus. This chapter is meant to continue, challenge, and widen the conversation and to provide hands-on tools to help you deepen these connections.

Sample Dialogues Connecting Service and Politics

The six sample dialogues below can help you lead discussions on the connections between service and politics. The dialogues address a range of topics:

Sample Dialogue 4-1: Exploring Service and Politics—What Is Your View?

Sample Dialogue 4-2: Connecting Service and Politics

Sample Dialogue 4-3: The Social Change Wheel

Sample Dialogue 4-4: Dialogue with Elected Officials

Sample Dialogue 4-5: Starfish Hurling and Community Service

Sample Dialogue 4-6: A Typology of Service Politics

Sample Dialogue 4-1: Exploring Service and Politics—What Is Your View?

Goal: To use a four-corners interactive format to discuss students' views on the connections between service and politics.

Introduction: As facilitator, have participants introduce themselves and tell a brief story about their involvement in service and/or politics (about 10 minutes). Explain the "four corners" format (below).

Activity—How do you feel about service and politics? Each of the four corners of the room should have a sign offering one of four options: *strongly agree, agree, disagree,* or *strongly disagree.* Read a statement about service and/or politics that is open ended and controversial enough to divide opinion somewhat evenly (see samples in the sidebar on this page). Have participants go to the corner of the room that best correlates with their position on the issue. If they are neutral, they can go to the center of the room. You will probably have to read the statement two or three times to allow people to think about their positions. In each corner, give participants a few minutes to discuss why they joined that particular group.

After five minutes, have the groups join in a large-group conversation. People can switch groups during the conversation if they change their minds. If anyone moves from one corner to another during the conversation, ask why.

Your facilitation is essential during this part of the dialogue. Try to facilitate a thoughtful conversation, not a debate. Keep in mind these tips:

- Go back and forth among the four groups.
- Ask people to wait to be called on so you can give everyone a chance to talk.
- Call on people who have not spoken before.
- Stop any back-and-forth arguments that might arise.

When conversation has been exhausted (depending on the size of the group, this might take about 10–15 minutes), ask if anyone has any final comments and then read a new statement and begin the process again.

You can use the four-corners format to facilitate conversation on almost any topic. It's important to craft statements carefully to make sure that you won't end up with everyone in the same corner. A good strategy is to test your statements among friends before using them in a dialogue.

Four-Corners Statements on Service and Politics

Following are some statements on service and politics that have worked well in four-corners conversations:

"Community service is a more effective strategy than political engagement for addressing problems in our society."

"Colleges and universities are more supportive of community service than of political participation."

"Community service should be required for graduation."

"Politicians value the voices and perspectives of college students."

"If more young people voted, it would transform American politics."

"National community service programs, like AmeriCorps, should continue not to allow participants to engage in any form of political participation (including nonpartisan voter registration) during their service hours."

Sample Dialogue 4-2: Connecting Service and Politics

Goals: To explore the connection between service and activism and to discuss the college or university's support for student public life.

Introduction: As a warm up, have participants introduce themselves and say one word they think of when they hear the word *service* and one word they think of when they hear the word *politics* (about 10 minutes). Then frame the dialogue by reading data on student political participation (see the sidebar below for some examples). Introduce the activities to follow by providing a tie-in to the statistics, such as: "Does this data provide an accurate picture? What can we do? In this dialogue, we hope to understand why there is this disconnect between service and politics. More important, we hope to come up with some recommendations for increasing the connection."

Activity 1—Your experiences with service and politics: Break the group into pairs. Have each person tell the other a story of something she or he has done recently that involved service and that involved politics (about 5 minutes, making sure each person has a chance to tell her or his stories).

After everyone has shared stories in the paired groups, reassemble in the larger group. Have the pairs share some of their conversations on service and politics (about 10 minutes). Framing questions may include: What are some examples of stories of service that you told? What are some examples of stories about politics? Were the stories different? If so, why do you think that? Was it difficult to think of stories about politics? Why or why not?

Activity 2—Ways to increase student political interest: Break into small groups for a discussion about why college students are increasingly involved in community service, yet decreasingly involved in politics and civic life. Is the statement accurate, from their experiences? Why aren't more students voting and participat-

---

Political Participation versus Service among Young People

- In the 2000 elections, 28% of all 18- to 24-year-olds voted, down from 42% in 1972 when 18-year-olds were first given the right to vote.
- In 2000, 26% of college freshmen voiced the belief that keeping up with politics is important, compared with 58% in 1966.
- Fewer than 20% of 18- to 29-year-olds say they are proud of how democracy works in the United States, compared with more than 50% of those 50 years old and older.
- Only 1 in 10 young people (aged 18 to 29) is able to name both of their U.S. Senators, compared with 1 in 3 of those over age 45.
- Involvement in community service is at an all-time high: almost 70% of young people report volunteering, belonging to an organization, or working to solve community problem.
- In a national survey, more than 82% of high school seniors reported that they engaged in frequent or occasional volunteer work that year.

Statistics drawn from Cynthia Gibson, "From Inspiration to Participation: A Review of Perspectives on Youth Civic Engagement." The Grantmaker Forum on Community and National Service, 2001. Available at www.pacefunders.org/publications/pubs/Moving%20Youth%20report%20REV3.pdf.

ing in politics? Then ask them to brainstorm ideas for how their college or university, public officials, and communities can increase interest in politics and voting among college students (about 15 minutes).

Reassemble in the big group so each of the smaller groups can present ideas for increasing student interest in politics and voting (about 20 minutes). Record these ideas on flip-chart paper. You can print and distribute them or and post them on a website later.

Wrap-up and action: Review the ideas briefly with the group to see which have the greatest support or highest priority. Call for a group of students to work with existing student organizations to develop a campaign to implement the strategies suggested.

Sample Dialogue 4-3: The Social Change Wheel

This dialogue, and the social change wheel on which it is based, was developed by Minnesota Campus Compact.

Goal: To have an interactive discussion about the various approaches to social change and analyze how to use multiple approaches to increase effectiveness in addressing a specific issue.

Introduction: As facilitator, tell participants that in the spirit of service-learning and experiential education, you are involving them in an exercise that will help them think more deeply about making a difference in communities. Explain that you're going to ask them to move to a continuum along the wall on which the two ends are labeled "Charitable Volunteer" and "Radical Social Activist." Tell them that the success of the exercise depends entirely on their participation and ask for their collective commitment to participate.

Activity 1—Where are you on the continuum? Ask participants to think about where they would place themselves on the continuum. Explain that some people will not fully understand or like the labels; participants should choose the appropriate spot based on their own understanding of what the terms mean. Reiterate several times that there is no "right" answer and state explicitly that for the exercise to work, they need to stick with the spot they have chosen, even if everyone else chooses the opposite end. Then have participants move to the spot they have chosen on the continuum.

Ask three people from one end of the continuum to explain their choice. You may need to ask some follow-up questions, such as, "How do you perceive the other end of the continuum?" "How would you describe the differences between this end of the continuum and that end?" Affirm whatever they say. You may want to paraphrase what they've said and then say, something like "Okay, so that was your perception of this or that end of the continuum," or "That's how you perceived each end." You want to ensure that everyone feels comfortable sharing their views, emphasizing that there is no right or wrong answer, only perceptions. Then have three people from the other end of the continuum do the same thing. Follow the process with three people from the middle of the continuum.

While participants are standing along the wall, emphasize the need for a range of approaches. Following are some suggestions for what to say:

> Any change movement must employ a number of strategies all along the continuum if it hopes to make change. For example, the Civil Rights movement is most often associated with protest politics and civil disobedience, but a big part of that movement were the Citizenship Schools that taught reading, writing, and skills for passing the citizenship exam—that is, direct service. There was also a tremendous amount of behind-the-scenes activity with politicians and others aimed at changing laws and providing support services such as job training. So we all need to think about not one strategy—charitable volunteerism or radical activism—that will make a difference, but rather about a set of strategies to solve the problem. We need both ends of the continuum and everything in between if we truly want to effect change.

> Too often, instead of working together, people at either end of the continuum chastise each other. Someone from this end [walk to the volunteer end of the wall] might say to those at the other end, "You all need to get real down there. You're never going to change the system. And while you're trying, more and more people who need help are falling through the cracks." Someone from this end [walk to the activist end] might respond, "You'll never make a difference one person at a time—the system itself has to change. You've got your finger in the dike while we're trying to stop the problem at the source." What's really needed is for the two ends—and everyone in between—to say, "How can we work together to make a real difference?"

Finally, ask participants what public participation strategies besides the two at each end of the continuum can be used to make change. If they don't come up with anything, mention formal political involvement, grassroots political involvement, and community/economic development efforts. At the end of the activity, ask for any final comments from participants, then thank them and have them sit down.

Activity 2—Making change: Segue from the first activity by asking, "What can we learn from what we just did about making change in communities?" Then hand out copies of the Social Change Wheel (see Figure 4-1) and ask for questions or comments. Is anyone involved in a program that uses a multifaceted approach to change? What you ask depends on the context and what you want the group to take away.

If you have time, or if you schedule a second meeting, you can ask the group to go into a detailed analysis of the Social Change Wheel, using a Depth Chart (see Figure 4-2) to look at activities that constitute "thick" or "thin" work within each strategy. (This activity is based in part on the work of Keith Morton [1995], who reviewed various paradigms for community involvement and suggested that the "integrity or depth" of such efforts was a key measure of their quality.) Have the group work through the following steps:

The group collectively identifies what activities or partnerships to consider and which category or categories on the Social Change Wheel those activities fall into (charitable volunteerism, etc.).

Individuals mark an "X" on the Depth Chart's thin-to-thick continuum, indicating their sense of the general quality of each type of activity, and write out comments related to the various elements they took into account in that rating. (Participants can do this on individual hard copies, which you as facilitator can transfer to flip-chart paper for the group to see, or they can simply mark their answers on a common chart, if they don't feel the need for anonymity.)

Participants discuss their assessments of each activity, including areas where they agreed and disagreed, as well as priorities and strategies for change in existing activities or partnerships in the future.

This process can uncover important issues and contribute to ongoing program improvement, as well as stronger relationships among stakeholders. The results of this process may also serve as a benchmark for future assessments.

Sample Dialogue 4-4: Dialogue with Elected Officials

Goal: To enable students to build relationships with elected officials through an interactive dialogue.

This sample dialogue offers a way to engage with elected officials by building relationships through dialogues. As facilitator, you can simply invite a politician to speak on campus so a large number of students can hear his or her views. These conversations can be panel discussions, speeches, or debates.

Another form of dialogue is to have a conversation with an elected representative or a team of representatives. The following model is based on a dialogue organized by the Johnson Foundation and Wisconsin Campus Compact, which allowed a small group of student leaders in service (with no interest in politics) to interact with two Wisconsin members of Congress in a moderated conversation. (See the sidebar on p. 115 for a description of the dialogue and the dialogue agenda.) This

FIGURE 4-1: **Social Change Wheel**

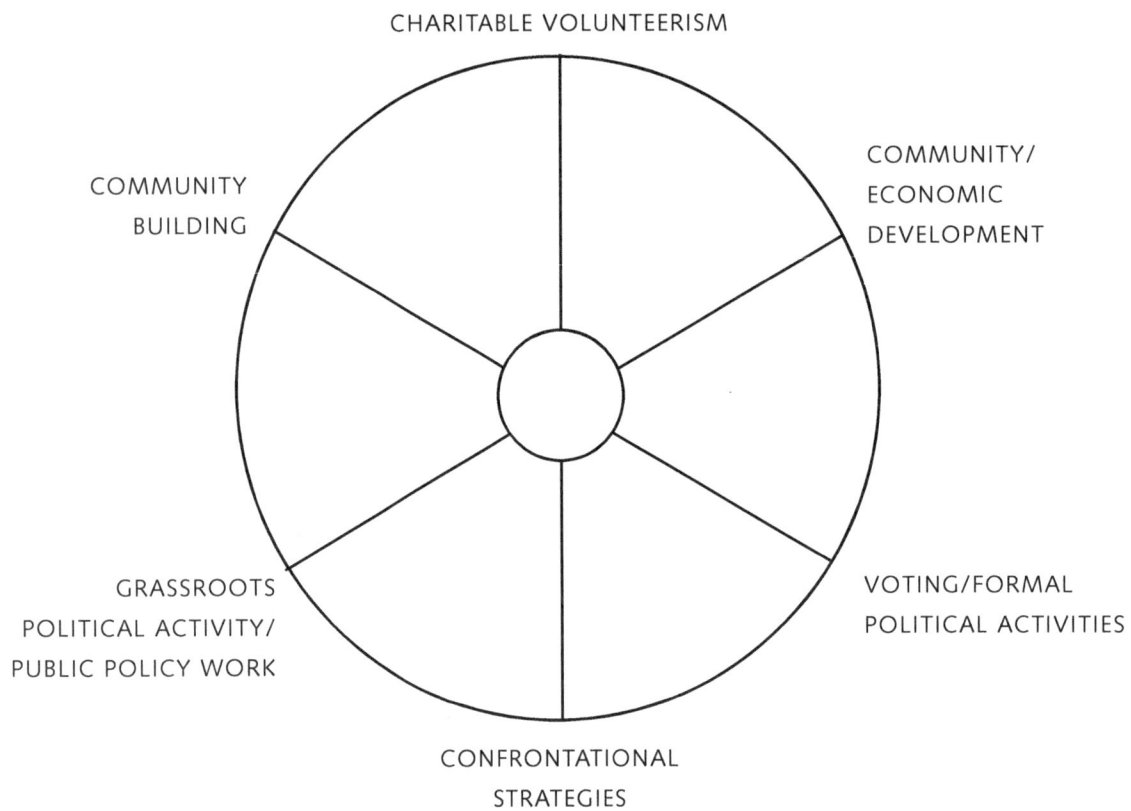

Examples

Charitable Volunteerism (activities that address immediate needs, but not the conditions from which these emerge): tutoring/mentoring children, serving food at a soup kitchen.

Community/Economic Development (activities that identify and increase the human and/or economic assets of a neighborhood/community): completing a neighborhood assets inventory to mobilize residents around the needs of children; assisting in job skill development for people who are homeless.

Voting/Formal Political Activities (activities that mobilize influence on public policy through formal political channels—campaign work, voting, voter registration): creating/distributing profiles of candidates regarding their records and stances on children's issues; coordinating voter registration of homeless adults.

© Minnesota Campus Compact, 1996.

Confrontational Strategies (activities that use confrontation or public disobedience as a strategy for raising awareness of or changing policy on an issue): organizing a rally demanding support for programs benefiting disadvantaged children; overfilling a public hearing with vociferous housing advocates.

Grassroots Political Activity/Public Policy Work (activities that help people identify allies, build common ground, and implement a strategy for changing public policy): organizing a letter-writing campaign urging Congress to preserve WIC funding; helping homeless people schedule meetings with local representatives.

Community Building (activities that build trusting relationships among individuals and groups around issues of common concern): involving kids, parents, neighborhood residents and college students/faculty in designing and building a playground or low-income housing.

SERVICE AND POLITICAL ENGAGEMENT

FIGURE 4-2: **Depth Chart**

	Charitable Volunteerism	Community/ Economic Development	Voting/ Formal Political Activities	Confrontational Strategies	Grassroots Political Activity/ Public Policy Work	Community Building
Thin						
Thick						

	"Thin"	"Thick"
Nature of relationship:	Placement	Partnership
Connection with other initiatives:	Isolated	Integrated
Approach:	Romantic/ recreational	Strategic/ change-oriented
Investment of resources:	Low	High
Stakeholder involvement:	Low	High

© Minnesota Campus Compact, 1997.

model includes a three-part process, with structured preparation and reflection before and after the event.

Preparation: Before the dialogue, invite students to meet to discuss expectations and prepare. Some questions you might ask include:

- How do you feel about politics or politicians?
- Why don't more young people vote?
- Do politicians address the issues of young people?
- What would a politician need to say or do to get young people more engaged?
- What do young people need to do to be taken more seriously by politicians?
- What do you expect to hear from the politicians?

Dialogue: For the dialogue, choose a respected, impartial moderator such as a professor on campus, a respected community activist, or the president of your college or university to facilitate. The moderator should have experience in that role and not be intimidated by an articulate politician. He or she should simply ask or prompt questions, keep the conversation open and respectful, and hold everyone in the dialogue responsible for answering the questions posed.

It can be helpful to set a theme or topic for the dialogue, although it's best to keep it broad enough to avoid focusing exclusively on one or two issues. For example, you might explore how students can be more politically engaged, what political/social issues students care about, or (as in the Wisconsin dialogue) how to connect service and the political process.

Reflection: After the dialogue, give students time to debrief, reflect, and plan for future actions. Some of the questions that might be addressed include:

- What was your initial reaction to the dialogue? (If the group is small enough, have everyone speak. If not, break into small groups.)
- Were there any surprises?
- Do you think the politician was being honest?
- Did you get past abstractions about politicians?
- Did your views change?
- What are the next steps?

Same Dialogue Agenda: Why Young Americans Hate Politics

DIALOGUE DESCRIPTION

In January 2004, college students from postsecondary institutions across Wisconsin were invited to join U.S. Representatives Tammy Baldwin and Mark Green at The Johnson Foundation's Wingspread Conference Center in Racine, Wisconsin. The purpose of the discussion was to explore the students' attitudes toward politics and their understanding of the connections between community service and involvement in the political process. *Washington Post* columnist E.J. Dionne moderated.

Wisconsin Public Television filmed the exchange and created a 25-minute video. (For a free copy of the video, see www.johnsonfdn.org/HorsesMouthVideo.html or email Kurt Wueker at kwueker@johnsonfdn.org.) Chris Beem of The Johnson Foundation has written a working paper for the Center for Information and Research on Civic Learning and Engagement (CIRCLE) about the event, with a review of the conversation and ramifications. The paper is available online at www.civicyouth.org/PopUps/WorkingPapers/WP27Beem.pdf.

DIALOGUE AGENDA
Thursday, January 8, 2004

10:30 a.m.	Introduction: Chris Beem, Program Officer, The Johnson Foundation
	Discussion: "What Do You Come With—Ideas, Preconceptions, Attitudes?"
	Facilitator: Nick Longo, National Student Coordinator, Campus Compact
12:15 p.m.	Lunch
1:30 p.m.	Panel Discussion:
	Moderator: E.J. Dionne, Jr., Columnist, *The Washington Post,* and Senior Fellow, Governmental Studies Program, The Brookings Institution
	Panel: United States Representative Mark Green (R-WI); United States Representative Tammy Baldwin (D-WI)
3:15 p.m.	Break
3:30 p.m.	Debriefing: "What Did You Hear? What Did You Think?"
	Group 1: Facilitator: Nick Longo
	Group 2: Facilitator: E.J. Dionne, Jr.
5:00 p.m.	Adjourn

Sample Dialogue 4-5: Starfish Hurling and Community Service

Goals: To probe conventional attitudes regarding community service and to think deliberately about effective service.

Introduction: Tell participants that you are going to hand out an essay meant to provoke dialogue about conventional attitudes toward community service. Note that at its core, it argues for being deeply connected to place and relationship; it argues for commitment to place and relationship as an alternative to have or have not or need-based models of service. The essay asks us to look carefully at the stories we choose to tell about our work—and to examine them for their assumptions and implications.

Activity—Attitudes toward service: As facilitator, have the group read Keith Morton's essay on "Starfish Hurling and Community Service" (see the handout in the sidebar on p. 117). After the group has read the essay, have each person spend five minutes writing her or his own response. In small groups (or all together if the group is small enough), allow each person to share her or his response. Facilitate a larger conversation about the issues raised by the essay. Ask questions about participants' experiences with service and whether their service sites address the criticisms in the essay. Suggest that the group respond to each of Morton's five criticisms.

In probing responses, ask people whether they have heard the starfish story before and if so, what their response was. Then ask them to respond emotionally and intellectually to the essay. Sometimes the essay angers people, but, when pressed, they most often find themselves agreeing with its five points. If you find this to be the case, ask them to explain where this dissonance comes from.

Wrap-up and action: Conclude by asking people to design a service project that meets the criteria set forth by Morton's advice:

> Don't go charging out to help. Talk, listen, build relationships, know your self, your environment; work with others where they and the situation itself can teach you how to act with more and more knowledge and effectiveness.

Sample Dialogue 4-6: A Typology of Service Politics

(Note: We recommend this dialogue as an activity for a student organization or class looking intensively at the service-politics connection. It is not intended for a one-time dialogue.)

Goal: To examine student roles and attitudes about politics, service, and service politics.

Handout for Dialogue 4-5: Starfish Hurling and Community Service

One of the most popular stories in community service events is that of the starfish: a [fill in your description, usually young] person is running, hurling starfish deposited on the beach by a storm back into the sea. "What are you doing," asks a [fill in your description, usually old] person, "you can't possibly throw all the starfish back. Your effort makes no difference." "It makes a difference to this one," replies the first person, and continues down the beach.

The usual conclusions drawn from this hackneyed tale are about the importance of making a difference where you can, one person or problem at a time; about not being put off by skepticism or criticism or cynicism. The story acknowledges the relief that comes when we find a way to relieve suffering. A somewhat deeper reading is that there is merit in jumping into a situation and finding a way to act—the first step in determining what possibilities for action might exist.

But the tale is, ultimately, mis-educative, and I wish people would stop using it. First, it is about a problem—starfish cast up by a storm—that is apolitical (unless you stretch for the connection between pollution and el Niño that might have precipitated the storm). There is seldom any hesitancy or moral complexity in responding to a crisis caused by natural disaster. It is the one circumstance in which charity can be an unmitigated good. The story suggests that all problems are similarly simple—that there is a path of action that is right and can avoid the traps of politics, context, or complex and contradictory human relationships.

Second, the story is about helping starfish and not about helping people. It avoids, therefore, the shadow side of the service, the sticky problem of who deserves our help. The starfish are passive; they have no voice; they cannot have an opinion about their circumstances, at least not that we can hear. This one is much like that one. Their silence coincides with the fact that they can have done nothing (the story suggests) to deserve their fate. In most of the situations where this story is told, service is about people working with people: people with histories, voices, opinions, judgment, more or less power.

Third, the story avoids the possible complexity of ecology: it might be that the starfish are part of a food chain that is being interrupted as they are thrown back—birds might go hungry at a critical time of year, for example; or it might be that the starfish have been released from the ocean bottom by a storm because they have outgrown their habitat. It is never smart to intervene in an ecosystem without understanding how all its parts are interrelated.

Fourth, the tale suggests that we should work from emotional response and not our heads, even though the problem is, in this case, a knowable one. As "overwhelming" as the miles of beach seem, the dilemma of the starfish is finite and knowable—this many starfish on this stretch of beach. A bit of advance organizing could result in enough volunteers to return all the starfish to the sea.

Fifth, the story privileges random, individual acts of kindness. It avoids questions of community (and we claim "community service" as our ground after all). It avoids questions of working with others. It polarizes the relationship of the two actors: How different would the story be if the second person joined in with the first?

In short, the story does nothing to teach us about community or service. This in itself is not necessarily a problem. It could be an entertaining tale, and that could be enough. What makes it a problem, however, is that the tale of the starfish pretends to teach us something about community service, even as it misdirects our sympathies, our intellects, and our sense of purpose.

Don't go charging out to help. Talk, listen, build relationships, know your self, and your environment. Work with others where they and the situation itself can teach you how to act with more and more knowledge and effectiveness. Stop hurling starfish.

Keith Morton, "Starfish Hurling and Community Service," *Campus Compact Reader,* May 2000, p. 23.

Introduction: As facilitator, have the group look at the chart outlining various aspects of politics, service, and service politics (see Table 4-1, below). The chart, which represents a typology of service politics, is a useful tool for reflecting on students' service experience.

Activities: The chart, which was developed for *The New Student Politics* Curriculum Guide (www.compact.org/students/curriculum_guide.html), can be a starting point for a series of discussions about civic engagement. For example, ask participants which box on the chart best describes the community service they undertake. They can then discuss why they chose the service they did. Use the following questions to encourage dialogue about civic engagement:

1. How do you define civic engagement?
2. How do you relate to conventional politics?
3. Do you see service as an alternative form of political action?
4. How do you translate your personal interests and issues into civic engagement?

TABLE 4-1: **Politics, Service, and Service Politics**

	Conventional Politics	**Community Service**	**Service Politics**
Student Role	Voter; consumer	Volunteer	Public problem-solver
Purpose	Provide policies, laws, and services, guarantee	Seek to alleviate immediate social needs	Connect individual acts of service to broader framework of systemic social change
Government is:	For the people	Of the people	By the people
Political Conception	Politics	Alternative to politics	Alternative politics
Goal	Promote individual interests	Address community needs	Promote community interests
Required Skills	Political knowledge, critical thinking, relationship building, negotiation	Relationship building, reflection	Awareness-raising, public problem solving, relationship and coalition building, community organizing, reflection, negotiation
Focus	Allocation of scarce resources	Geared toward symptoms (immediate needs)	Looks at systems (structural change) and root causes of problems

5. Do you consider democracy to be inclusive and accessible? If not, how could it be?
6. How has service-learning bridged your service work with politics?
7. Are the activities and the mission of your campus aligned with the values of inclusion, justice, reciprocity, community building, and participatory democracy?
8. What kind of input and agency do students on your campus have in shaping civic engagement on campus?
9. Are students on your campus seen as active producers (as opposed to consumers) of knowledge and democracy?
10. Do you view your service activity as political in nature? Is your service an example of service politics? If so, how? If not, why not?

Additional questions that probe participants' attitudes and actions more deeply might include:

1. Why do you participate in community service?
2. In what ways has your service increased your commitment to addressing particular social issues and to the community in which you serve?
3. Do you see a disconnect between your campus and the community that surrounds it?
4. If you wanted to make a change on campus, how would you go about doing so?
5. If you wanted to address an issue or policy that affects your community, how would you do so?

By the end of the dialogue, try to get the group to define their understanding of service politics and develop ways to make stronger connections between the various approaches.

Service Politics and Alternative Breaks

Increasingly, students are using breaks in the academic year to work with a community, usually away from their campus. These trips are called "alternative" breaks because of the contrast with the stereotypical spring break with students vacationing at the beach. The primary goals of an alternative break trip, as outlined by Sarah Seames (2005), are to:

- Bring together a group of students to become a team
- Learn about a specific issue facing a community and methods for improving it

- Provide a needed service to a community
- Experience personal and group growth through reflection

Every year, thousands of college students choose alternative breaks. However, the trips are often criticized for not being challenging in a deep, meaningful way. Skeptics ask, "How can one week truly make a difference?" and, "Are students really gaining knowledge about the issues they are working on or just providing a 'hit and run' form of service?"

The strategy of college administrators and student leaders is to provide a quality experience complete with proper preparation, community education, appropriate service, and in-depth reflection. With all these elements in place, students can experience a new understanding of social issues and a dedication to making change that lasts long after the experience.

Students involved with Raise Your Voice took alternative break trips one step farther by incorporating the campaign's philosophy that students can and do make change through any number of methods, including direct service, education, activism, and political engagement. Trips included visits to state houses to meet with local and state officials in more than a dozen states, as well as to Washington, DC. The latter trips typically combined direct service in a particular area with education on relevant issues, reflection, dialogue, and meetings with national legislators. (See the section called "Plan an Alternative Spring Break Trip to Washington, DC," on p. 122, for details.)

The objective of these trips was to illustrate to students that they can make a difference on an issue through whatever method feels most appropriate for them. The trips also illustrated the connections between direct service, which many of the students were accustomed to performing, and the policies that are determined by those in power. One student noted, "This trip was amazingly inspiring. Actually visiting DC taught me a lot because of the relatively close locations of so many volunteer opportunities, delegations, lobbyists, and our capital. Visiting our delegation dissipated my grandiose views of Washington and Congress. Now I feel comfortable with visiting, writing, and lobbying because I had this positive experience."

Planning an Alternative Break Trip

Alternative break trips include many elements. Following is a brief list of factors to consider when planning a trip. More information on alternative breaks is available from Break Away, a nonprofit organization that supports the development of alternative break programs, at www.alternativebreaks.org.

SITE AND ACTIVITY DEVELOPMENT

The first order of business is to select a site for your trip. Consider how far you want to travel, what type of service you want to do, how the site will affect your budget, and the site's experience working with volunteers. Be sure that your site has accommodations for you, and make plans for bringing or acquiring provisions. This is particularly important for relief efforts; for example, many Gulf Coast areas affected by Hurricane Katrina did not have the infrastructure after the storm to support an influx of volunteers.

BUDGET

Create a budget so that you know how much money you will need to raise for the trip. The budget should include travel, lodging, any site fee, and provisions. Some schools pay for the cost of the trip, some require participants to raise all needed money, and some provide part of the money while participants raise the rest.

TRIP AGENDA

What do you want to *do* on the trip? Besides the obvious direct service, consider including at least one civic element. Some possibilities follow. (More information on combining service and politics on the trip appears in the next section.)

Education. Build in time for participants to become more informed about the issue you're working on. You may, for example, schedule a meeting with a community-based organization in the area you are serving to find out more about homelessness.

Lobbying or policy change. Plan to meet with your Congressional delegation if in DC, or local politicians, if elsewhere. Tell them about the service you are performing and discuss specific bills or policies that you'd like them to act on. (You'll need to schedule these meetings as early as possible in the planning process.)

Dialogue. Contact community groups or local high school or college student groups in the area that you'll be serving and set up a dialogue with them. Discuss the issue you're working on, its root causes, and the different ways to effect change.

Keep in mind that alternative break agendas are never set in stone. Trip leaders must adjust the schedule based on changing meeting times, the weather, and the mood of the group.

STUDENT RECRUITMENT

Be creative in recruiting students. Make unusual posters. Utilize campus email announcements or listservs. Have students or trip leaders announce the trip in classes. Put displays around campus with pictures of previous trips. Try to appeal to different types of people; tell them about the various activities that will take place on the trip. Make sure that students understand all the requirements of the trip (participant fee, pre-trip meetings, no-alcohol policy, etc.).

PRE-TRIP MEETINGS

After you've recruited your group, meet with them regularly. In these meetings, plan various activities, including team-building and icebreaker activities, education on the issue you'll be working on, logistics and paperwork (e.g., health forms, trip agreements, liability release), and group decision making (e.g., what to do with time off, planning meals). Ensure that participants understand that the meetings are a requirement of the trip. Make it possible for everyone to have a good experience. Develop a plan for dealing someone who signs up for the trip but doesn't attend the meetings.

REFLECTION

As with any type of community service, reflection is an important component of an alternative break trip. Reflection allows participants to process what they've experienced and learn from each other. Make plans for daily reflection to be part of the trip. An ongoing group journal is one way to record the events of the trip and give participants a way to reflect and communicate with the group. (For more information on alternative break reflection, see Seames, 2005, in the references at the end of this chapter.)

POST-TRIP FOLLOW-UP

Follow-up with participants after the trip should be part of the initial planning process. Many participants will want additional ways to remain involved. Set a date for a trip reunion beforehand so that participants know when they'll be able to get back together. Plan to provide follow-up materials such as information on local issues related to the trip activities, places where participants can volunteer at home, and a copy of the group's journal.

Strategies for Incorporating Political Engagement

Incorporating other civic elements into community service in alternative break trips helps participants better understand the issue on which they are working. By including a public policy dimension, you can show students another way to make change on a social issue that they may not have considered before or may have been intimidated to try. Following are several methods for incorporating political action into traditional alternative break programs.

PLAN AN ALTERNATIVE BREAK TRIP TO WASHINGTON, DC

The nation's capital offers a unique setting that includes direct service providers, advocacy organizations, and the United States Congress. Design an alternative break trip that includes direct service, education, and meeting with your U.S. Congressional delegation. Have a specific issue or bill to discuss that relates to

SERVICE AND POLITICAL ENGAGEMENT

your service work. Make sure participants are well informed about the issues on the table, and be prepared to outline and defend a clear course of action. It is also useful to include reflection time in the schedule to give participants a chance to talk about their service experiences and to connect those experiences with policy issues.

In 2003, Maine Campus Compact brought students from seven Maine colleges and universities to Washington, DC, to work on hunger and homelessness issues. Their work included volunteering for food banks and other local organizations as well as meeting with lobbying groups and Congressional staff members. (See the sidebar on p. 124 for the trip's agenda.)

The following year, Maine Campus Compact and Campus Compact for New Hampshire organized another alternative break to Washington, DC, this time to work on environmental issues. Students volunteered with environmental organizations and attended workshops on fair trade and lobbying. This time, they were able to meet directly with their Senators and Representatives to speak about their volunteer work and discuss current legislation and environmental issues.

PLAN A LOCAL ALTERNATIVE BREAK
Although alternative breaks usually involve travel, local communities may offer an excellent chance to build long-term relationships that have a lasting impact. In addition, local sites may help recruit students who otherwise would be unable to go on an alternative break trip because of financial or time considerations. Design a program that gives students the opportunity to work locally during the break, so that they do not have to leave their responsibilities at home behind. If your campus is within a reasonable distance of your state capital, plan a day to meet with your state representatives regarding the service you've been providing during the week.

If you choose a local site, try to connect with one or more local organizations with which you can continue to work in the future. You may want to plan a series of shorter "trips" rather than one longer one. For example, Ross Meyer, a student at Miami University in Ohio, created a weekend program for students to work in the local Over-the-Rhine community that remains ongoing four years later (Meyer, 2006).

UTILIZE PRE- AND POST-TRIP MEETINGS
At pre-trip meetings, discuss the issue you'll be working on during the week and what local, state or national policies affect this issue. Invite local politicians who may be working on this issue to speak at one of your meetings. At your post-trip meeting/reunion, have participants write letters to their representatives about their experiences on the trip and any related legislation they'd like the representa-

Agenda—Alternative Spring Break Trip to Washington, DC

This agenda is from Maine Campus Compact's 2003 "Drive for Hunger and Homelessness" alternative break trip.

Monday, February 17

9:00 – 12:30	Volunteer at D.C. Central Kitchen
1:00 – 4:00	Group A – Volunteer at Capital Area Food Bank
	Group B – Volunteer at Martha's Table
7:00 – 8:00	Reflection

Tuesday, February 18

7:00 – 12:00	Volunteer at So Others Might Eat
1:00 – 4:00	Group A – Volunteer at Martha's Table
	Group B – Volunteer at Capital Area Food Bank
7:00 – 8:00	Reflection

Wednesday, February 19

9:00 – 12:00	Volunteer and meet with Bread for the World
3:00 – 4:30	Faces of Homelessness panel
7:00 – 8:00	Reflection

Thursday, February 20

9:00 – 10:30	Meet with National Coalition for the Homeless to receive lobbying training
11:00 – 12:00	Capitol Hill tour
1:00 – 1:30	Meeting at Congressman Michaud's office
2:00 – 2:30	Meeting at Congressman Allen's office
3:00 – 3:30	Meeting at Senator Collins' office
4:00 – 4:30	Meeting at Senator Snowe's office
7:00 – 8:00	Reflection

Friday, February 21

8:30 – 9:45	Present at American University class
2:00 – 5:00	Hunger and Homelessness dialogue
6:00 – 8:00	Writing Reflection Workshop

tive to take action on. Other possible meeting activities are outlined in the next section.

GET EDUCATED

Research local advocacy organizations related to the issue you're working on (for example, the local HUD office) and set up a meeting with a representative from the organization specifically to discuss policy related to their work. If possible, connect with more than one organization to get a range of perspectives and to address issues from multiple angles. For example, a recent spring break trip organized by the University of Louisiana System involved not only working with Habitat for Humanity to rebuild housing but also meeting with the Red Cross to learn about disaster relief and preparedness. In addition, the group joined with Louisiana Campus Compact to seek ways to increase the impact of their efforts through ongoing policy and service work.

MEET WITH LOCAL REPRESENTATIVES AFTER RETURNING

Before leaving, set up a meeting with a local or state representative to discuss the issue you are working on once you return. Discuss the upcoming meeting with participants both during and after the trip. Have participants research local, state, and/or federal legislation related to the area of service to discuss at the meeting.

ORGANIZE A CAMPUS EVENT

Have students organize a related event on campus upon their return. Possibilities include displays around campus; a dialogue or speaker on the issue you've worked on; an article in school newspaper; or a letter-writing campaign targeting local or national officials.

Pre- and Post-Trip Meeting Activities

EXAMINING PRIVILEGE

(Note: This activity requires a facilitator with experience in managing group reflection. It is best done after the group has met a few times and completed group-building activities.)

Put the numbers 1 through 10 along a wall. Ask students to stand by the number that represents how much privilege they think they've had in their life (1 is no privilege and 10 is the most privileged). Explain the various elements of culture, life, and upbringing that they may use as a basis for their decisions (see the list in the sidebar that follows). Begin with relatively simple, non-threatening areas and gradually move to more sensitive, personal ones. After each item, ask participants to explain why they are standing

Elements of Privilege

How much privilege do you have, based on:

- The country you were born or live in
- Your gender
- Your age
- Your family's or your income level
- The language(s) you speak
- Your family's structure (parents together, divorced, etc.)
- Your education
- Your religious affiliation
- Your skin color
- Your sexual orientation

where they are. In this activity, it is important to tell people that they do not have to reveal anything about themselves that they do not wish to. No one should be forced to speak or share.

EXPLORING CAREERS FOR THE COMMON GOOD

Have participants think about the careers that make a difference in the world and write each on a piece of paper (5 minutes). Have them share their thoughts with the group. Then ask a few volunteers to arrange the jobs into categories. Categories may include health care, public service, education, and so on. Write the categories on pieces of paper that you put up around the room. Ask the participants the following questions; after each one, and ask them to stand by the category that best answers the question for them. Then have them explain their choices.

- What type of career do you think is the best way to make a difference for an individual?
- What type of career do you think is the best way to make a difference for society?
- What type of career do you think is the least effective way to make a difference?
- Which type of career do you think you are most likely to pursue?
- Do you think you can make a difference in any career you pursue?

RANKING CIVIC ENGAGEMENT ACTIVITIES

Once you have an idea of what you will do on the break trip, create a form that lists each activity of which the group will be a part (e.g., volunteer work, policy/lobbying training, reflection, dialogue, meeting with legislative staff). Have participants rank the items based on which ones they think will make the most difference. After participants have ranked the items on their own, have them share their rankings and their reasoning.

Try this activity both before and after the trip to see if participants change their opinions about the best way to make a difference.

Contacting Your Legislator

(Note: Most of this section and the following section on "Other Forms of Political Action" were adapted from Sarah Seames, *Back to Basics: A Guide for College Students to Understand and Participate in the Political System*, Maine Campus Compact and the Points of Light Foundation, 2005.)

Legislators represent the districts they serve and want input and direction from the voters. While it's impossible for them to fulfill the requests of each individual, they do take into account the input they get from their constituents. There are several methods for contacting your senator or representative, including writing letters, emailing, calling, and visiting. This section provides guidance on each method. Use these tips as a guide, but don't feel that you have to follow them exactly. Do what feels right and fits best with what you are seeking to accomplish.

A note on lobbying: Lobbying is often thought of as something done by large corporations to influence legislation that could affect their profits. But lobbying can include any activities aimed at influencing public officials and/or legislation. Lobbying can be done by individual citizens and should be thought of as a basic right. Don't cringe at the sound of the word; be proud that you are utilizing your rights as a citizen if you lobby your legislator on an issue that you care about.

Writing and Calling

LETTERS

Letter-writing is one of the most common, effective ways of contacting a legislator. When a constituent takes the time to write a letter, it shows that the issue is of great importance to them. Legislators often assume that the person who wrote the letter represents many more people with the same view who don't have the time or initiative to write. According to a report by three nonprofit/activist groups (Oxfam America, COOL, and Bread for the World, *Just Add Consciousness*, p. 2), "Congressional staff members say all it takes are 10 to 20 handwritten letters to draw their attention to an issue." To have the greatest impact, organize a letter writing campaign, although don't discount the value of an individual letter.

Here are some tips to consider when writing to a representative or senator about a specific issue or bill:

- Properly address the person you are writing to. Members of the House of Representative should be referred to as Congressman, Congresswoman, or Representative. Members of the Senate are Senator.

- If possible, write your letter by hand. This personal touch tells the legislator that it is not a form letter. Make sure it is legible.

- Write about only one issue per letter and try to keep it to one page. Be sure to keep your tone respectful.

- Thank the recipient for any past support he or she has given on the issue you are writing about.

- Do your homework. Refer to any legislation related to the issue by name and number. You can find such information at www.congress.gov or www.vote-smart.org. State how you'd like the recipient to vote on the specific bill.

- Include personal examples and stories illustrating how the bill will affect the representative or senator's district. Give pertinent facts and figures, but don't overwhelm with numbers.

- Mention groups and communities you're a part of and make it clear that you're a constituent.

- Include any pertinent attachments—informational documents, news articles, letters to the editor, etc.

- Request a response that outlines their position on the issue or bill. Give your address in the body of the letter; envelopes are often discarded.

- If the response is noncommittal, write again asking the legislator to clarify his or her position.

- Have at least one person proofread your letter before you send it. You lose credibility if your letter has grammar or spelling mistakes.

EMAILS

While email is often the most convenient way to contact your representative or senator, it may be the least effective. Email is seen as impersonal and used for mass-production campaigns of form letters. If you email your legislator, be sure to make it personal. All the same rules and advice for letter writing apply to emails. Some additional tips to consider include:

- Do not use form letters from advocacy organizations. Write in your own words and make it personal.

- Do not attach anything to your email. Fear of viruses could prevent someone from opening it.

- Include your mailing address in the email so your legislator can respond.

PHONE CALLS

Calling your legislator is an easy, quick way to urge them to act. It is particularly useful in the days leading up to a vote on a bill, when there may not be enough time to send a handwritten letter. A phone call is a personal way of contacting your senator or representative, although it often doesn't allow you the time to fully explain your reasoning and position on an issue. You can find the phone numbers for the members of the U.S. Congress at www.house.gov and www.senate.gov. When calling a member of Congress, consider the following:

- Know the name and bill number of any legislation related to the issue you are calling about. Check on the status of the bill before you call.

- Know the voting history of your legislator on this issue.

- Identify yourself and any affiliation you may have.

- If you don't have much time, leave a message with the person who answers the phone. Be sure to tell them your name, that you're a constituent, your contact information, and how you'd like your legislator to vote on the upcoming bill.

- If you have the time, ask to speak with the legislative aide who works on the issue you're calling about.

- When speaking to an aide, tell him or her the reasons for the position you hold. Provide pertinent facts and figures and explain how the bill will affect the legislator's district, giving personal stories when possible.

- Offer to send any background information you have soon after the conversation.

- Ask the position of the senator or representative and request a response in writing.

- Be sure to thank the person you speak with.

Meeting in Person

Perhaps the most effective way to convey your position or message to a legislator is by meeting with him or her personally. Whether in Washington, DC, at your state capital, or at an event elsewhere, a face-to-face meeting can be powerful. If you are planning to be in DC, set up a meeting with your senator or representative ahead of time. If no legislators are available, meet with the legislative aide who works on the issue you are interested in. Aides help keep legislators informed about current issues and bills and can be very influential in helping to set your legislator's stance on a piece of legislation.

It is important to recognize that meeting with Congressional staff members can be just as fruitful as meeting with the legislator in person—and is considerably more likely to happen. Even if you are scheduled to meet with a senator or congressperson, it is possible that a schedule change may land you with a staff member instead. You should be prepared either way to speak about your service experience and lobby around any related legislation. Making a good impression with a staff person can not only help your cause but also help pave the way for a future meeting with the legislator.

Following are some tips on setting up, preparing for, and meeting with legislators or their aides. (See the sidebar at the end of this section for what to avoid when talking with Congressional staff.)

SCHEDULING THE MEETING
- Set up the meeting at least two weeks in advance and confirm the date and time a few days ahead of time.

- Call the office of the legislator and ask for his or her scheduler. You can find the phone numbers of your U.S. representatives at www.house.gov and senators at www.senate.gov.

- Tell the scheduler who you are and how many people you will be bringing to the meeting. Be sure to state that you're a constituent. Be specific about the topic of the meeting and ask to meet with both the legislator and the legislative aide who works on the issue you'll be discussing.

- If possible, note any specific legislation that you'd like to discuss. Have the name and bill number available.

- Some schedulers may ask you to send the request in writing. Do so if asked, but follow up with a phone call if you don't hear back promptly. Be persistent!

PREPARING FOR THE MEETING

- Research the issue you'll be discussing and find out the name, number, and status of any current related legislation. You do not need to be an expert on the topic, but you do need to know the basics.

- Prepare a one-page summary of the issue and your position to leave with the legislator. Be sure to include the name and number of the bill in question, if there is one.

- If you're going with a group, choose a spokesperson who will introduce the group and your purpose. Prepare a brief description of your organization or group.

- With the group, decide who will say what in the meeting. This will ensure that you cover the main points and that more than one person speaks.

- Think about your legislator's position on the issue and prepare responses to possible arguments.

- Practice the visit. It may seem awkward, but rehearsing what each person will say in the meeting helps immensely. You'll feel confident about what you're going to say and you can clear up any confusion ahead of time.

- Assign at least one person to take notes during the meeting.

- Plan to dress appropriately. Professional dress is expected at Capitol Hill, so no T-shirts or jeans. Suits for both men and women are ideal, but if you don't have a suit professional-looking pants or skirts are fine.

- Bring a map of Capitol Hill. Maps can be found at www.senate.gov in the Visiting section.

MAKING THE MOST OF THE MEETING

- Arrive early and allow plenty of time to find the office of the legislator. In Washington, DC, the House and Senate office buildings can be confusing.

- Be flexible. Schedules change constantly for members of Congress, so don't be surprised if your meeting gets pushed back or shortened. If the senator or representative can't meet with you because of a schedule change, have your meeting with a legislative aide. Your message, information, and request will still get to the legislator.

- Bring information on the issue or bill, including your contact information. A one-page summary is ideal; be sure not to bring too much paper that requires a lot of reading time.

- You will not have much time with the legislator, so get right to the point. Give a brief overview of who you are and why you are there. Then make the request that you came for. Tell the senator or representative what action you want him or her to take and why.

- Explain the issue or bill as concisely as possible.

- Include a personal story of how this issue has affected you, someone in your group, or someone you know.

- Relate the issue to the district the legislator serves. Explain how it's affecting his or her home town or state and how the residents there feel about it.

- Thank the legislator for any past support he or she has given on this issue; avoid any criticism of past votes.

- Ask for a response, even if it has to come later in writing.

- Be sure to take notes of the meeting, especially any questions the legislator or aide asks that you don't know the answer to. Tell them that you will find out and get back to them, and do so promptly. Never, ever lie or guess at an answer. They don't expect you to be an expert, and you'll lose their respect if you are not truthful.

- Be respectful of their time and wrap up the meeting promptly.

- Invite them to any upcoming events you're organizing in their district and offer to be of further assistance to them on the issue you've talked about.

- Take a picture with the legislator before you leave.

FOLLOWING UP

- Send a thank you letter. Include the major points of your conversation.

- Find out the answers to any questions the legislator or aide asked that you didn't know at the time. Send the information promptly.

- Invite them again to any upcoming events in their district.
- Keep track of their action on the issue you spoke about. Make sure that they vote the way they promised to. Write to them after any votes related to the issue and thank them for their vote or ask them why they voted the way that they did.
- Write to and meet with them in the future on other issues you care about.

Examples: Student Visits to the State Capitol

Over the past three years, students across the nation have been participating in "Days at the State House" as a way to engage their peers and policymakers. By presenting resolutions, lobbying, and having conversations with elected officials, students are making their voices heard on vital public issues. When they make a statement, become engaged, and recognize the stake that they have in their own futures is when others begin to notice.

Students from Illinois, Maine, Michigan, Montana, Oklahoma, and West Virginia drafted and presented student-written "public issue statements" at their state houses, describing the responsibilities of young people and the support necessary from institutions to engage their peers. These students said that higher education needs to support and nurture students' political development, and asked for specific legislative support. Other students have addressed specific issues such as hunger and homelessness in their states. In some states, visits to the state capitol have become an annual event.

Visits to the state capitol have been effective for engaging student peers and elected officials in various ways. Some examples follow.

OKLAHOMA LUNCHEON WITH THE GOVERNOR

To kick off a Week of Action, students from Oklahoma met with the governor, state legislators, and college presidents at the state capitol to present a public issue statement about their commitment to civic engagement. The statement, which was designed to leverage support for the issue of youth civic engagement with state policy makers and college administrators, reads in part:

> We declare that it is our responsibility to become an engaged generation with the support of our political leaders, education institutions, and society.... The mission of our state higher education institutions should be to educate future citizens about their civic as well as professional duties. We urge our institutions to prioritize and implement civic education in the classroom, in research, and in service to the community.

Oklahoma Governor Brad Henry responded by issuing a declaration proclaiming it "National Student Civic Engagement Week—A Week of Action" in Oklahoma.

Top 10 Things Congressional Staff Hate to Hear

Number 10: But I thought my appointment was with the Senator!

Never, ever indicate that you are disappointed to be meeting with a staff person. Having a good relationship with a staff person can make or break your cause.

Number 9: Here's some reading material for you: our new 300-page annual report!

When meeting with a member of Congress or staff person, limit the materials you leave behind to one or two pages, and include details on where the information can be found on the web, if appropriate. Offering the information in a file folder with your organization's name on the label will help ensure that the materials are put in a file drawer, as opposed to the circular file.

Number 8: How much of a campaign contribution did your boss get to vote against (or for) this bill?

Most staff have little or no idea who contributed to their boss's campaigns. Not only is this question insulting, but even if it were accurate, the staff person isn't likely to know.

Number 7: I assume you know all about our bill, HR 1234.

With thousands of bills introduced during each Congress, no staff person will be able to keep them all straight. Always provide information on the bill title, number, and general provisions when communicating with a Congressional office.

Number 6: No, I don't have an appointment, but I'll only take half an hour of your time.

Unless it's an emergency, or you are good friends with the staff person, try not to engage in the much-dreaded "stop by." Most staff are happy to set up a meeting if you are relevant to the office (i.e., you are a constituent). Even if you have an appointment, don't expect a full half hour.

Number 5: No, I don't really need anything specific.

If you don't ask for something specific, like co-sponsorship of a bill, a Congressional Record statement, or a meeting in the district, staff will wonder why you came by. Updates on your program are fine, so long as they are accompanied by a request. That will ensure that someone in the office thinks about you and your request for longer than five minutes. According to one Congressional legislative director, "Constituents who contact me with workable great solutions to local problems always get my attention and frequently influence our decisions and policymaking efforts."

Number 4: We have 10 (or more) people in our group who would like to meet with you.

Congressional offices are tiny. If you have more than five people in your group, you'll likely be standing out in the hallway. Plus, having so many people talking at once dilutes the impact of your message.

Number 3: What you're telling me can't be right. I heard [fill in name of talk show host] say otherwise.

Most staff or members won't lie to you. They may see things differently than you do, but if they say a bill definitely is not going to be considered on the floor or no such legislation exists, believe them.

Number 2: What do you mean we have to stand in the hall?

See number 4. A request to meet in the hallway is simply an indication of space limitations. Nothing else.

Number 1: I don't represent anyone from your district. I just thought you'd be interested in what I have to say.

Your time is always best spent working with your own elected officials and turning them into advocates for your cause.

(SOURCE: Adapted from the American Youth Policy Forum. Used by permission.)

MICHIGAN STUDENT PROPOSALS
Michigan Campus Compact set up a legislative hearing where college students could present new ideas for bills. Nine students presented their ideas, and many legislators spoke individually with particular students whose ideas they were interested in sponsoring. Several of those students continued working with legislators and their staff to draft the proposals.

TEXAS RESOLUTION ON STUDENT CIVIC ENGAGEMENT
Campus Compact coordinated training of student leaders and staff coordinators from 13 colleges and universities in Texas. Each team planned a series of civic events for their campuses, which were held during the Week of Action. On February 24, 2003, at the Texas State House, students met with the lieutenant governor, the speaker of the house, and their legislators. They also introduced a concurrent resolution supporting student civic engagement in the House and Senate.

INDIANA DAY AT THE STATE HOUSE
Indiana college students from across the state spent February 17, 2003, at the state house meeting legislators, getting a tour and overview of state government, and seeing each chamber in action. They also learned more about Indiana's Unified State Plan for Service, learned how to get more involved in their community, and presented their views on how to engage students in service and on other related issues.

MISSOURI STUDENT-LEGISLATOR DIALOGUE
On February 20, 2003, Raise Your Voice and Missouri Campus Compact sponsored a student-led dialogue at the Missouri state capitol with hundreds of college students along with their legislators and the lieutenant governor. The dialogues focused on the questions: "What civic issues are important to students?" and "What are students doing to address these concerns?" Students reported on their dialogues on the floor of the state house.

Other Forms of Political Action

Although contacting your legislators may be the most direct form of political action, many other options are available for raising the awareness of students (and others) about public policy issues that affect communities. Following are a few examples.

Invite a legislator to an event or service project. What better way to get a politician to understand what you're talking about than to have him or her see it firsthand? Invite the politician to a service project or event that you're hosting as a part of the event, not just a token speaker.

Testify in front of a committee. When a bill has been introduced and referred to committee, that committee may hold a hearing to gather further information on the issue or bill. Contact your legislator to find out how or if you can testify at the hearing.

Organize an issue forum or dialogue. You can bring the issue you are working on to the attention of those on your campus or in your community by hosting a forum or dialogue. A dialogue is a public space where people can discuss a topic and try to find common ground. Provide information to the participants on any current legislation related to the topic. (For more information on how to organize and facilitate a dialogue, see Chapter 3, or go to www.actionforchange.org/dialogues.)

Sponsor or organize a debate. Invite politicians or advocates on an issue to debate on campus or discuss a certain issue or piece of legislation. Provide information to the audience on how they can contact their legislator to support or oppose the bill.

Coordinate a petition or signature drive. A petition shows your elected officials that many people support or oppose a piece of legislation. Ensure that signers give their addresses to prove they are constituents.

Organize a teach-in. A teach-in is any event that gives participants information on an issue or skills on how to act on the issue. Teach-ins may take the form of speakers, video presentations, workshops, or conferences.

Participate in a demonstration. A demonstration is a way to support (rally) or oppose (protest) an issue or bill in a public way. It is intended to draw attention. Different forms of demonstrations include vigils, sit-ins, marches, pickets, and silent protests. Whatever form you choose, keep it peaceful. Violence detracts from your message and can be counterproductive.

Volunteer on a political campaign. If you strongly support a candidate, you can volunteer on his or her campaign. You may also work to get a particular referendum passed or defeated. On a campaign, volunteers help in many ways, including putting up signs, assembling mailings, phoning, going door to door to talk to voters, and working on websites.

Organize a voter registration drive. If you'd like to see more students vote, you can organize a voter registration drive on your campus or in your community. Get a voter registration kit from Rock the Vote at www.rockthevote.com.

Write a letter to the editor. Letters to the editor are an easy way to reach many people. You can discuss an issue of concern or a current piece of legislation. Most papers have length limits, so check the website of your local paper before you write. Make sure to have someone proofread it before you send it.

Donate money. You can donate money to support particular candidates, a political party, or nonprofit organizations that work on issues you care about. Some (although not all) of these donations are tax deductible.

Run for office. Get into the action yourself and run for political office. Age requirements vary from state to state and office to office. Contact your town hall or state house for more information on how to run for office.

Creating Hubs for Civic Engagement

A number of colleges and universities have made an institutional commitment to exploring and promoting a wide range of civic engagement strategies. It can be helpful to learn about their programs as you seek to establish, expand, or refine work on your own campus. The examples listed below are just a few of the institutions that are advancing student civic engagement by connecting service with social advocacy and democratic participation. More information is available on the websites listed.

COLGATE UNIVERSITY
Center for Outreach, Volunteerism, and Education (COVE)
The COVE, East Hall
13 Oak Drive
Hamilton, NY 13346
http://offices.colgate.edu/cove/default.htm

COVE is Colgate's center for service, citizenship, and community building. COVE conducts team-based service work with a public work orientation. It challenges simplistic volunteerism by deliberately connecting service with community building and democratic engagement.

MIAMI DADE COLLEGE
Center for Community Involvement
300 NE 2nd Avenue
Room 1452
Miami, FL 33132
www.mdc.edu/cci

Miami Dade College, the largest community college in the country, uses student leaders in service and civic/political engagement as an integral component of the service-learning program.

MIAMI UNIVERSITY OF OHIO

Office of Service-Learning and Civic Leadership
Social Action Center
Oxford, Ohio 45056
www.units.muohio.edu/saf/service

The Social Action Center (SAC) was developed by student leaders at Miami University to connect direct service groups with advocacy groups on campus. Housed at the Office of Service-Learning and Civic Leadership, SAC promotes collaboration through training, resource sharing, and ongoing dialogue among student organizations.

UNIVERSITY OF PENNSYLVANIA

Center for Community Partnerships
133 South 36th Street, Suite 519
Philadelphia, PA 19104
www.upenn.edu/ccp

Civic House
3914 Locust Walk
Philadelphia, PA 19104
www.vpul.upenn.edu/civichouse

The Center for Community Partnerships has become a national leader for its efforts to engage in campus-community partnerships through the academic curriculum. These partnerships are part of an ongoing commitment to West Philadelphia and therefore involve both direct service and political organizing. Civic House develops mostly co-curricular, student-led initiatives that connect community service with social advocacy work.

UNIVERSITY OF UTAH

Lowell Bennion Community Service Center
200 Central Campus Drive
Salt Lake City, UT 84112
www.sa.utah.edu/bennion

The University of Utah's Bennion Center has developed a new, student-initiated program called Service-Politics and Civic Engagement (SPACE) that connects an impressive group of service-learning programs. Through SPACE, students address controversial issues and are creating an integrated program that connects service and politics to make systematic change.

References

Beem, C. (2005). *From the horse's mouth: A dialogue between politicians and college students.* CIRCLE Working Paper 27. (Available at www.civicyouth.org/PopUps/WorkingPapers/WP27Beem.pdf.)

Dionne, E.J. (2000). *Effective citizenship and the spirit of our time.* Paper prepared for the Surdna Foundation.

Gibson, C. (2001). *From inspiration to participation: A review of perspectives on youth civic engagement.* Berkeley, CA: The Grantmaker Forum on Community and National Service.

Long, S.E. (2002). *The new student politics: The wingspread statement on student civic engagement.* Providence, RI: Campus Compact.

Meyer, R. (2006). Social action at Miami University: Lessons from building service-learning. In Zlotkowski, E., Longo, N.V., and Williams, J.R., *Students as colleagues: Expanding the circle of service-learning leadership.* Providence, RI: Campus Compact.

Morton, K. (1995). The irony of service: Charity, project, and social change in service-learning. *Michigan Journal of Community Service Learning, 2*(1), 19–32.

Morton, K. (2000, May). Starfish hurling and community service. *Campus Compact Reader, 1*(1), 23.

Oxfam America, Campus Opportunity Outreach League, and Bread for the World. (n.d.). *Just add consciousness: A guide to social activism.* (Available at www.uiowa.edu/~c07e161a/AdvocacyGuide2000.pdf.)

Seames, S. (2005). *Back to basics: A guide for college students to understand and participate in the political system.* Lewiston, ME: Maine Campus Compact and The Points of Light Foundation.

Seames, S. (2005). *A guide to leading reflection in alternative break programming.* Lewiston, ME: Maine Campus Compact and The Points of Light Foundation. (Available at www.uma.edu/communityengagement/Documents/Sarah%20Seames%20Legacy%20Project.doc.)

appendix
Training the Trainers

This final section provides training materials for student leaders, faculty, staff, and others interested in training other students to take on a leadership role. The training resources are based on the activities and information in the preceding chapters. Included are several sample training sessions, including trainings on preparing to make change, community mapping, and creating dialogues, as well as an on examining lessons from your own past work.

This last training discussion includes an overview of Campus Compact's Raise Your Voice "Lessons Learned" retreat in 2004, in which students reflected on best practices over the previous three years of student action on hundreds of campuses nationwide. To help you recreate a similar examination, we provide the meeting's agenda and a description of students' efforts to capture and disseminate results from the retreat.

In the spirit of this guidebook, the material in this section is meant to encourage you to think creatively, but it also offers concrete examples for you to use or adapt as appropriate. Use what is helpful to prepare for your work on campus; as with all organizing work, however, the best way to see what works is to get started, revising and reflecting as you go. We hope these resources give you more confidence to claim your power as students on campus.

Sample Training A-1:
Preparing Students for Making Change on Campus

This type of training can take many forms. In the Raise Your Voice initiative, we have used the framework below along with the dialogue on "How Students Are Creating an Engaged Campus" (see Sample Dialogue 3-7 in Chapter 3). If you have time, we suggest using this combined approach both to give students a broad picture.

As facilitator, ask participants to give their name, school, and what they are doing or want to do to change their campuses. Share why you feel the need to talk about participants' goals and the goals for the training. (Here is where you can incorporate Sample Dialogue 3-7, if time allows.)

Tell participants to think about a continuum based on how much power they have to make change on their campus. The physical continuum is indicated with tape on the floor; one end is labeled *powerless* and the other *power to influence change.* After everyone has moved to a place on the continuum, pick a few people standing in different areas and ask them why they've chosen that particular spot. Delve deeper into the dynamics of campuses by asking questions such as: "For those who have made change on your campus, what were the most important elements? What allowed you to be a change agent? What resources did you mobilize?" Write all the answers on flip-chart paper to summarize them at the end.

Ask people to pair up and tell a story about a time when they felt powerful on campus. Have people stay in pairs and ask a few to tell their stories. Then ask each pair to find another pair, ideally others who might be doing similar work. Ask them to think about these questions: Who are the three most important people you need with you to influence the change you want to make? What four critical strategies can students use to build power on campus?

Have the small group report and list their answers (allies, resources, strategies) on the flip-chart paper, adding to the items already there. Conclude by steering people to resources on campus, in the state, or online.

Sample Training A-2: Community Mapping on Campus

(Note: Definitions and activities from this sample training are adapted from the Asset-Based Community Development Institute and the Center for Democracy and Citizenship at the University of Minnesota.)

For many students, mapping is the starting point for their organization or project. It is a way to get a sense of what's already happening on campus and what gaps exist. (See the mapping guide in Chapter 2 for more information on this process.)

To introduce this topic, in a large group, ask, "What comes to mind when I say the words: *asset, power, mapping?*" Share associations from each word and write responses on flip-chart paper. Make connections from these associations to what mapping is and can be used for. Talk about the importance of both the process and the product.

Several types of mapping may be useful:

- **Self-mapping:** Who do I know? Who am I connected to? What are my skills and assets?
- **Group mapping:** mapping relationships and networks.

- **Asset mapping:** identifying a community's existing assets and resources.
- **Power mapping:** creating a map of resources, authority, and decision-making ability in a given organization, campus, etc.

Mapping Skills Sets and Networks

This activity is intended to establish the skill sets needed for the leadership group working on your project. It is only one way of using mapping; do not feel the need to replicate it exactly.

Ask the group to think visually, using a "spider diagram" to map skills and networks that may of use in doing engaged work (see the Community Mapping Tool in Chapter 2). It may be helpful to use the idea of having a web of support as a metaphor. Divide participants into small groups. Each group should have many pieces of colored paper. Ask each participant to do a separate spider diagram mapping: 1) individual skills, talents, and passions; and 2) networks and associations.

Have each person list three skills, talents, or passions individually on pieces of paper, and then do the same with three networks or associations. Each person should put these six pieces of paper in the middle of the table. Ask each group to share a few of the items with others in their group. Then have all of the groups bring their pieces of paper to one central place for you to read and discuss (you can also ask groups to call out examples and write them on a flip-chart). Talk about how this list represents underlying assets and networks that can be leveraged. It may also be useful to have each small group to try to pair skills and networks together as a way to demonstrate how to make connections from mapping.

Identifying Uses of Mapping

Ask the group for ideas on how they can use mapping on their campus. Remind them that different types of mapping provide different data. Share stories of other students who have used mapping for a variety of purposes, such as:

- To find gaps in services and identify community need.
- To identify individuals doing similar work in order to build recruitment or support.
- To determine student groups doing civic engagement work in order to avoid overlap and find synergies.

Finally, write the following steps in the mapping process on flip-chart paper so participants can see the progression:

1. **Develop goals**—Talk to the group about their goals for mapping, such as to develop new knowledge or relationships while balancing interests and community needs (tell your own story here, if you can).

2. **Identify an ally**—Ask each person to identify an ally they might use for a mapping process such as another student, your community service director, a faculty member, or someone who can help you think about navigating your campus. Ask the group for examples of who they would target as an ally.

3. **Plan the process**—Ask each person to consider what process they will use, who will do what, and how much time will they need.

4. **Follow up**—Remind the group of steps to take after the planning process:
    - Start the mapping process: conduct interviews, stop by offices, look at literature, hold dialogues and personal conversations
    - Check in with allies and others
    - Take action: What are you going to do with this information?

To help student leaders understand the mapping process, do a sample mapping activity by asking, What is helping and hindering student engagement on your campus? (See the Help/Hinder chart in Chapter 2.)

Sample Training A-3: Dialogues

With the group, discuss how mapping can lead to a need for dialogue and make the dialogue more successful by identifying the right people to participate (decision makers, potential advocates). Dialogue can also be a tool for mapping; even informal discussions can identify those who are interested in a particular issue or activity.

Ask the group to think about the last time they discussed a community or public issue with someone (who was it, what issue, when was it, how did it start and end). Each person should find someone they do not know and take five minutes to share stories. In the large group, ask for a few examples. Make the point that in a democracy, we need to be able to talk about things in a safe, respectful way and change the culture of social issues from debate to dialogue.

Purposes of Dialogue

Ask the group these questions: What is a dialogue? Why is it a big part of Raise Your Voice initiative? Put the reasons to hold a dialogue on a flip-chart pad for reference. For example:

A dialogue…

…brings together people from diverse backgrounds and experience.

…opens avenues for discussion, learning, and cooperation.

…promotes understanding of different points of view.

…identifies information or issues.

…offers opportunities for people to become part of a network of active and concerned citizens.

…explores diverse views and ideas, giving participants a range of alternatives for further thought.

Share the following reasons for holding dialogues on campus and ask the group for additional ideas:

- People want to hear what students have to say.
- Students should be comfortable using their voices and having their own perspectives.
- Dialogues create safe, democratic, respectful space for students to discuss issues that matter to them.
- Dialogues promote student knowledge, service, and action.

Preparing Dialogue Leaders

Ask the group to think about their own current work and how it can help them in creating an overall plan. Have a group discussion. Encourage the group to think about whether they want to organize a process-oriented (end) or goal-oriented (means) dialogue. Ask for examples or refer to stories told earlier. Talk about how this decision plays into factors such as whether to have a one-time event or coordinate sustained activity, what format to use, and how formal or informal you want the dialogue to be.

Go over the planning process for the dialogue. Remind the group to consider format (open issue, guided issue, town hall meeting, public policy dialogue, learning circle) and other aspects of planning, such as size, participants, space, recording, publicity, and facilitation. (Note: For this section, we recommend referring to the information on planning and facilitating a dialogue, in Chapter 3.)

Think about who will facilitate the dialogue and what roles each person will play. Then go over the components of facilitation (you may also want to put them on flip-chart paper):

- Introduction, welcome, ground rules
- Topic framing: why you're there, goals
- Dialogue launch: ice breaker

- Discussion/activities: strategies for keeping the conversation going
- Wrap-up: review of what's been said, where participants want to go, available options
- Action steps: How did it go? What are you doing with the experience?

In conclusion, stress that facilitation is often the most critical component of a dialogue. Unprepared facilitators can be accused of wasting valuable time; strong facilitators have the ability to make sure that everyone participated and got something out of the discussion. Ask for questions. You may also want to have those present share any stories from their own experience about what did or didn't work well in past dialogues.

Creating Sample Dialogues

It can be helpful in training dialogue leaders to have them gain experience by creating sample dialogues. Explain the purposes of the activity: to try out this process, to practice facilitating, and to develop sample dialogues that may be used on campus.

Break the group into pairs and ask them to develop a sample dialogue, including the topic, goal or objective, format, participants, how to introduce it, and questions that guide the dialogue. Have each group put their dialogues on flip-chart paper (20 minutes). While they are working, visit each group and identify one pair to lead the larger group in reviewing their sample dialogue.

When each pair is done, have everyone reassemble and ask the group you identified to try out their dialogue (20 minutes). Then hold group reflections on the dialogue to review what worked (10 minutes). Share the other dialogues participants developed (10 minutes). Ask if anyone has ideas for using these sample dialogues on campus.

Sample Training A-4: Hosting a "Lessons Learned" Gathering

The three-day national Raise Your Voice conference in 2004 proved to be a highly effective venue for reflecting and reporting on the most effective strategies for student organizing on campus (see the Lessons Learned declaration in Chapter 1). You may want to work with other student leaders, faculty, administrators, and staff to recreate a local version of this meeting to capture the lessons learned from a service program, political action, or organizing project on campus. The process can also be used to capture student voice on a host of issues on campuses and in communities. (See the conference agenda in the sidebar at the end of this section for ideas about how to structure such as meeting.)

The Chicago conference was led by students, who planned, participated in, and documented the gathering. However, it also required institutional support, as well as guidance and support from staff at Campus Compact. The planning process involved five groups of participants: a student and staff planning team, student participants, staff participants, invited guests, and a student writing team.

The Team

Student and staff planning team. The planning team of five students and three staff members was organized so that the students led the process and the staff helped with logistics. To recreate this team, we recommend forming a team with a mix of students and staff or faculty. Ideally, staff and faculty support the students in developing the format, substance, and approach of the meeting. Students should outnumber staff and faculty on the planning team.

Student participants. The planning team invited Raise Your Voice student leaders from across the country to submit applications to attend the Lessons Learned conference. The application included a one-page essay on "What lessons have you learned from Raise Your Voice?" A group of students and staff then selected 30 participants on the basis of their essays. (Note: These essays also helped to document valuable lessons and plan the gathering.)

In recreating a similar event, we recommend that you decide on your audience and keep the gathering small for maximum interaction, whether you use a selection process or an invitation-only process. At the same time, to ensure a range of ideas and viewpoints, recruit for racial, ethnic, and gender diversity, as well as for diversity of experiences.

Staff participants. Approximately 12 staff members involved with Raise Your Voice were invited to participate in the conversation. We recommend that key staff, faculty, and administrators on campus and community partners be invited to participate. This group should be substantially smaller than the student group (at least two students for each non-student).

Invited guests. Certain key stakeholders, such as funders and scholars, were also invited to attend and listen to the conversation. We recommend that the planning group map key stakeholders on campus and invite a selected group.

Student writing team. Campus Compact sent out a job description to choose students who attended the meeting to document and write a publication based on the conversation. The team members moved to Providence, RI, to write the document collaboratively over the following summer. This paid internship also included a learning circle and a series of brown bag lunches at which they reflected on issues. We recommend that this model be used to hire students (possibly over the summer) to write up the lessons from programs, organizing, and projects from the perspective of students themselves. Other options include course credit through an independent study for students on the writing team.

The Logistics

Setting. The Lessons Learned gathering was held at a retreat center in Chicago over three days, which allowed one full day when no one was arriving or leaving. Participants were required to attend the entire gathering. No one could arrive late or leave early out of respect for the group and to ensure continuity of the conversation. A retreat setting is ideal. If you can, take your group off campus for several days. If this is impossible, we suggest asking participants to commit to attending the on-campus event for the entire duration.

Capturing the lessons. In Chicago, group conversations were recorded on flipchart paper; scribes took notes in the large and small groups. In addition, to capture participants' views more intensively, the planners allowed time for taped interviews with a small group of participants. The planning team developed the essential questions and facilitated the interviews. The interviewers used the same set of initial questions but then followed up with additional questions based on the responses they received.

We recommend you have someone take notes during the gathering. Whether you record part of the conversation or do interviews depends on the time and resources you have. One of the most time-consuming aspects of capturing the meeting is listening to and transcribing the tape recordings, so if you tape, build time into the agenda. As you plan the agenda, constantly ask, "How are we going to capture this section of the discussion?"

Follow-up. The Lessons Learned conference has led to a Lessons Learned publication (Germond, Love, Moran, Moses, & Raill, 2006), a series of online toolkits, a host of organizing activities, and the development of local, state, and national relationships among student leaders. We recommend that you be clear from the beginning about the goals of your meeting and then work to have concrete products and follow-up from the event.

Sample Agenda—Raise Your Voice "Lessons Learned" Conference, Chicago, IL

Day 1 (Friday)

5:00–6:00	Introduction and icebreaker Goals of the gathering
6:00–7:00	Dinner and student speaker
7:00–8:30	Playback Theater: A reflection activity about your experience with RYV with an acting troupe from Chicago
8:30–9:00	Small-group discussions: Your experience in working with RYV

Day 2 (Saturday)

8:00–9:00	Breakfast
9:00–9:15	Conversations in pairs: Your definition of civic engagement and where it has led you
9:15–10:15	Large-group debrief
10:15–10:30	Break
10:30–11:30	Small-group discussions: Successes and obstacles in RYV work
11:30–12:15	Small-group presentations
12:30–1:30	Lunch

1:30–5:35	Student interviews and group workshops
	
	    1:30–2:45 Session A
	
	    2:55–4:10 Session B
	
	    4:20–5:35 Session C
	
	Students and staff organizers will be interviewed during one of the sessions and attend workshops during the other two sessions. A 15-minute break will be included in the interview session.

6:00–7:00	Dinner
7:00–9:00	Open space technology

(continued next page)

Day 3 (Sunday)

8:00–9:00	Breakfast
9:00–10:15	Small-group discussions: What can Campus Compact do to further its support of students? What can your college do to support students?
10:15–10:30	Break
10:30–11:15	Large-group debrief
11:15–12:00	Large-group discussion: How will we communicate these lessons?
12:00	Conclusion
12:30–1:00	Lunch

Reference

Germond, T., Love, E., Moran, L., Moses, S., & Raill, S. (2006). *Lessons learned on the road to student civic engagement.* Providence, RI: Campus Compact.